PROFESSOR BIRDSONG'S

"365"
Weird Criminal Law
Stories for Every Day
of the Year

Leonard Birdsong
Winghurst Publications

The Florida Authors and Publishers Association Award recognizes book publishing excellence and creativity in design, content, and production for North American authors and publishers.

On Saturday, August 9, 2014 Professor Leonard Birdsong won an award for one of the best eBooks of the year.

Professor Birdsong's "365" Weird Criminal Law Stories for Every Day of the Year
by Leonard Birdsong

© 2014 (Kindle), 2016 (paperback) Leonard Birdsong

ISBN: 978-0-9972964-0-2

Winghurst Publications
1969 S. Alafaya Trail / Suite 303
Orlando, FL 32828-8732
www.BirdsongsLaw.com
lbirdsong@barry.edu

Disclaimer:
The facts that are recounted in the stories in this volume are true and in the public domain, as best as Professor Birdsong can determine from his research of court documents, newspapers, and wire services. The author's commentaries on these stories are his own views and opinions and do not reflect the official policy or position of any Law school, Law firm or other organization with which the author may be affiliated. The opinions provided herein are not intended to malign or defame any religion, ethnic group, club, organization, company, individual or anyone or anything. The author further covenants and represents that the work contains no matter that will incite prejudice, amount to an invasion of privacy, be libelous, obscene or otherwise unlawful or which infringe upon any proprietary interest at common law, trademark, trade secret, patent or copyright. The author is the sole proprietor of the work and all parts thereof.

Permissions:
Cover graphic:
©seamartini|Dreamstime.com, ©Violka08|Dreamstime.com, ©Albund|Dreamstime.com

Book cover design: Rik Feeney / www.RickFeeney.com

TABLE OF CONTENTS

Professor Leonard Birdsong

Introduction

Professor Leonard Birdsong lives in Orlando, Florida where he teaches Criminal Law, White Collar Crime, Evidence, and Immigration Law. He has written many scholarly legal pieces since joining the legal academy.

Professor Birdsong writes in the areas of the Criminal Law, Death Penalty Law, Evidence, and Refugee Law. A number of U.S. courts have cited Professor Birdsong's scholarly pieces in their opinions: including the state Supreme Courts of Idaho, Illinois, New Jersey and Utah.

This work that you have purchased is not one of those scholarly pieces!

This volume of Professor Birdsong's Weird Criminal Law Stories is written just for fun and enjoyment. This time around he brings you his "365" Weird Criminal Law: Stories for Each Day of the Year. He hopes it will bring you laughs all year long.

Professor Birdsong has been involved in serious criminal law work over the years as a federal prosecutor, a defense attorney, and a law professor, However, he knows that it is good to get a good laugh at least once every day. That is why several years ago he began to collect and edit from the wire services and news the types of weird and funny criminal law stories that appear in this volume.

Professor Birdsong wishes to thank his brilliant student research assistants, Erin Sperger, Carissa Aponte and Megan Fletcher, for all of their editorial assistance on this volume of stories.

You may find other volumes of *Professor Birdsong's Weird Criminal Law Stories* at Amazon.com, *or* by going to his website: Leonard Birdsong.com.

Enjoy!

Stories for January

JANUARY 1

FLORIDA: The power of Christ commands you! Police in the town of Holiday arrested a 54-year-old man after a fight with his 80-year-old live in girlfriend got out of hand and he attempted to perform an exorcism on her. David Benes held her down and told her he was trying to "get the devil out of her."

JANUARY 2

CZECH REPUBLIC: Petr Svacha, 26, is facing a possible year in jail after using a chainsaw to slice his way back into a restaurant in the town of Zlin after closing time. Svacha just wanted to finish eating his pudding. Waiters at the restaurant had kicked Svacha out midway through his dessert because the restaurant was closing for the night. ...Must have been some really good pudding!

JANUARY 3

BRAZIL: Prisoners in Brazil have a new way to win early release – knitting. The cons at Arisvaldo de Campos Pires prison are being allowed to perform work knitting clothes for a local fashion designer. The prisoners get a day shaved off their sentence for every three days of knitting. Do they really want convicts to have knitting needles?

JANUARY 4

FLORIDA: Yep, that's her story and she is sticking with it. The bomb squad in Jensen Beach was shocked to learn that the suspicious package they were set to dismantle was only a sex toy. "It was a pink plastic adult novelty item, with some type of a plastic rabbit attached to it," the sheriff told reporters. The woman who received the package maintained she never ordered it.

JANUARY 5

NEW YORK CITY: An ex-marine who plotted to behead Federal Judge Joseph Bianco and a prosecutor – to avenge his Ponzi scheme convicted buddy, sobbed and begged a Brooklyn federal judge to "give him a second chance in life, that's all I am asking," he said at sentencing. Judge John Keenan was not moved and sentenced Djevid Mirkovic, 38, to 24 years in prison. An appropriate sentence for plotting to behead a federal judge, crybaby!

JANUARY 6

INDIA: Four men were arrested for trying to smuggle $100,000 in gold into the country – in their stomachs. The men had swallowed a banquet of small gold bars and coins to avoid customs. That's $25,000 in each of them. Wonder what would've happened if one of them had to take a dump?

JANUARY 7

ARIZONA: Police on underage drinking patrol singled out a father at a Cardinals NFL preseason football game that had asked his fifteen year old son to hold his beer while the father took photographs of the action on the field. The police officers kicked the whole family out of the stadium, and state liquor officials said that if they had been stricter, the father could have received two years in jail. OK, some states have just become ridiculous with their anti-alcohol campaigns.

JANUARY 8

NEW MEXICO: A violent woman was arrested after police said she attacked her boyfriend with a boot, a tire iron and a screwdriver – while he was behind the wheel with car moving. The Dona Ana County Sheriff's Office says the suspect is being held in jail on battery charges. The boyfriend must have cheated on her and she found out about it!

JANUARY 9

GEORGIA: a Newton County sheriff's deputy crossed the line and allegedly started selling marijuana out of his patrol car. Deputy Darrell Mathis allegedly told a pal that he would never be caught because he was police officer. Unfortunately, he was wrong. The pal went to the FBI. There's a song titled "A Policeman's Work is Never Done," but this policeman's job is certainly finished.

JANUARY 10

OREGON: It was easy for authorities to discover the counterfeit $20 bills that Michael Dietrich allegedly turned out. Why? Well, they all had the same serial number. His lack of imagination was discovered by a gun dealer in the town of Keizer who spotted the duplicate 20's. This case is even weirder because at the time of Dietrich's arrest he was the manager of the Oregon State Department of Revenue. Perhaps, he was not paid enough at the Department of Revenue!

JANUARY 11

FLORIDA: Welfare fraud? Welfare Queen? Ashley McGinley, 23, was arrested for selling food stamps on her Facebook page. Hernando County sheriff's deputies had no problems catching her – she was already in jail on other unrelated charges.

JANUARY 12

PENNSYLVANIA: A thief with a heart of gold? Nine year old Jaiden Newcomer who lives in York won a 250 pound pumpkin at an Oktoberfest celebration. He proudly kept the big pumpkin on his front porch before someone stole it. The thieves then later returned the pumpkin with a note that read: "I'm sorry about taking your pumpkin. Sincerest apologies."

JANUARY 13

CALIFORNIA: What a perv! Downloading child pornography may be sick but there are times such people should not download. Here is an example: Walter Gafvert III of Boulder Creek, was picked up on suspicion of possessing thousands of child porn photos. While he was being questioned, Santa Cruz detectives looked at his cell phone in his hand and found that it was actively downloading child porn.

JANUARY 14

CHINA: It appears that that there are a tremendous amount of smokers in China. How do we know? When officials at Beijing's Palace Museum, aka, the Forbidden City, began enforcing a smoking ban by confiscating cigarette lighters, 8,0000 were taken away the first day of the ban. This just burns me up…

JANUARY 15

TEXAS: Jailers have issued new charges against inmate Paul Reyes, 32, for allegedly possessing a contraband cell phone while locked up in the Bexar County. Sheriff's deputies received a tip that Reyes was taking pictures of himself behind bars and posting them to Facebook. Jailers found the phone in his pants and the charger around his waist. Sounds like a case of "selfie" incrimination.

JANUARY 16

TEXAS: Police in Lewisville did not have to go to great lengths to arrest two men on felony theft charges. Why not? The crime took place at police headquarters. The suspects were in charge of the criminal evidence section at headquarters and over a three year period they, allegedly, stole items, including: tools, a knife, a camera, and thousands of dollars in cash. Buzzards....

JANUARY 17

FLORIDA: An 80-year-old man wearing lipstick was arrested in Ocala for allegedly swiping a woman's purse and other items. Security guards saw the man, who wore blush and bright red lipstick but no wig, tearing price tags off items and stashing them into a purse which he had not paid for. The man tried to get away without paying – yet, he had $800 in his wallet. There's no coot like an old coot!

JANUARY 18

TEXAS: We hear that the Texas "panty robber" has struck again. For the last two years the "panty robber" has been breaking into East Texas homes and taking only women's undergarments. The Angelina County Sheriff's Department recently reported the latest burglary wherein, for the first time, the "panty robber" also took children's underwear. Yep, we now have pervert on the loose in East Texas!

JANUARY 19

CALIFORNIA: Reporters make the news! Two 19-year-old thugs approached Jeff Bush, a reporter for KRON-TV, and demanded his equipment. Bush's bodyguard opened fire on the would be muggers, wounding one of them and leading to their arrests. Attacks on TV news crews have been on the rise. Prompting Bay Area stations to send armed security to shadow reporters.

JANUARY 20

TENNNESSEE: A murder conviction was overturned and a new trial ordered when it was revealed that one of the jurors "friended" one of the expert witnesses on Facebook and sent a message complimenting her testimony. This online error helped accused murderer, William Smith, get a new trial. D'OH!

JANUARY 21

IDAHO: Exposing himself like that was not much of a political platform! James "Jimmy" Brown a city councilman from Spirit Lake was arrested for allegedly exposing himself to a woman during an angry confrontation with her husband, authorities report. Councilman Brown and the man were arguing outside of a tavern when the lawmaker allegedly displayed his genitals and shouted, "This is what a real man looks like!"

JANUARY 22

CALIFORNIA: Zaaaaaaaap...A burglar recently broke into a California Edison station in Pico Rivera to steal valuable copper wiring and touched a breaker, knocking out power and himself. He was found semiconscious with burns on one arm. We learn he will be charged with burglary as soon as he recovers.

JANUARY 23

INDIA: Police in India are in a spot of trouble for arresting a man for drinking a cup of tea in a "suspicious" manner. Vijay Patil, 49, was sipping chai at a roadside stall when officers handcuffed him and took him to the police station. A Bombay court quashed the charges, calling them "bewildering" after police claimed the man didn't give a good explanation for his tea drinking habits. Sometimes Indians are more British than the British about their tea drinking.

JANUARY 24

ARIZONA: Stephen Chapman, 22, of Pinal County, was found in bed with a wayward spouse. When her husband showed up, Chapman refused to leave the couple's home. It is reported that Chapman allegedly charged at the shotgun toting husband, who then shot his wife's lover in the hand. However, when police showed up at the house, it was Chapman who was arrested, on suspicion of disorderly conduct. He should have been arrested for stupidity!

JANUARY 25

CONNECTICUT: UGH! Campus police at Yale are hunting for a nasty person who they call the "poopetrator." The person has been wreaking havoc at the Ivy League school by defecating inside dryers in a student laundry room. His or her scheme was discovered only after victims finished drying their clothes and found them covered with "evidence."

JANUARY 26

OKLAHOMA: The headline read: "The Burglar's crime really stank." A burglar was arrested by police in Oklahoma City after he stopped to take a dump in the homeowner's bathroom and forgot to flush the toilet. Detectives obtained a DNA sample from feces that was left on toilet paper and linked it to Charles Williams, 20.

JANUARY 27

MICHIGAN: A judge in Lansing fined a cell phone user for contempt of court. Judge Hugh Clarke, Jr. fined himself $50 after his own cell phone rang during a sentencing hearing. He said his integrity was at stake after he had ordered everyone in attendance to turn off their cell phones. Ironic, no?

JANUARY 28

ITALY: Italian long distance runner Devis Licciardi was accused of using a fake penis to deliver "clean" urine after a 10K race to beat doping allegations. We've heard that the fake penis is called a "whizzanator."

JANUARY 29

GEORGIA: I don't give fine tine! We learn that police in Statesboro have found the town's beloved "fork in the road." The 7-foot-tall, 150 pound steel sculpture had stood as a bolted down landmark for a local business whose owner would direct customers to "look for the fork in the road." The fork was found leaning on a telephone pole outside of town.

JANUARY 30

MICHIGAN: Grade school fight club? A female custodian at Campus Elementary School in Grand Rapids was fired for allegedly offering to pay two fourth graders $1 each to beat up another student. The targeted student had allegedly made disparaging remarks about the custodian.

JANUARY 31

CALIFORNIA: A Los Angeles pornography producer has agreed to never again use Ben & Jerry's ice cream flavors for the titles of his xxx-rated films, court documents revealed. After being sued a year ago, Caballero Video agreed to recall and destroy films it had been distributing under titles like "Hairy Garcia," "Boston Cream thigh," and "Peanut Butter D-Cups. Sort of makes one not want to eat Ben & Jerry's ice cream anymore

Stories for February

FEBRUARY 1

NEBRASKA: Cheeky? You know you are dealing with a special type of vandal when his calling card is leaving behind a greasy butt-print. For more than a year, an unknown bandit has been pressing his naked behind – smeared with lotion or petroleum jelly – on the windows of businesses in tiny Valentine Nebraska. "This is the weirdest case I've ever seen," said Police Chief Ben McBride.

FEBRUARY 2

FLORIDA: Charity begins at home. A Florida elementary school student tried to pay for lunch with a counterfeit $20 bill, one of dozens another student had been handing out. In all, the eight year old passed out $880 in phony money, but officials say it is unclear where he obtained the currency. Of course, his parents, who police discovered had criminal records, were arrested.

FEBRUARY 3

WASHINGTON STATE: A marriage off to a rocky Balboa start? A Washington woman was arrested for allegedly beating up her fiancé at their prenuptial party when her son caught him making out with one of her friends. Police say the woman tackled and punched him and broke his glasses. There is no word on whether the wedding was still on.

FEBRUARY 4

FLORIDA: Drinking and floating do not mix. A drunken Tampa man passed out on a pool float at a Tampa beach and drifted a mile out into the Gulf of Mexico. The Coast Guard rescued the man, who was still unconscious when rescuers got to him.

FEBRUARY 5

FLORIDA: Transferred intent! Cesar Villazano, age 19 was sentenced to life in prison for fatally shooting a cross-dressing male outside a Daytona Beach nightclub one year ago. Villazano was found guilty of second degree murder when he shot and killed Mario Oscar Mosqueda. Testimony at trial revealed that Villazano was trying to pick up another cross-dressing (unnamed) male outside the dance club that caters to a gay and cross-dressing crowd. The unnamed cross-dresser spurned Villazano's advances. Villazano, in a fit of anger, opened fire at him with a handgun, missing the intended target but striking Mosqueda in the back of his head.

FEBRUARY 6

INDIANA: Some find God in different ways. Police in Elkhart who busted up a meth lab in Elkhart found the chemist's recipe for making the meth mix hidden inside a bible. Another lab was found in the same building two months earlier, after an explosion.

FEBRUARY 7

CALIFORNIA: Potty pyros beware — Clorox is looking to clean you up. Someone has been setting construction site toilets on fire since November, 2008, causing $50,000 in damage. The cleaning chemical company is offering a $5,000 reward and a year's supply of toilet cleanser for tip-offs leading to the arrest of the toilet torcher.

FEBRUARY 8

NEW YORK CITY: OUCH! A 17-year-old victim who was riding a Manhattan subway at 10:45 on a weekday morning was asked for the time by a young thug. When the 17 year old ignored him and proceeded to get off the train the mugger snatched his ipod. When the teen demanded it back, the thug pulled out a hypodermic needle and stabbed him in the stomach. The youth was tested for HIV but test results were not yet available. The stabber remains at large.

FEBRUARY 9

MARYLAND: Easter is over, sister! Prosecutors in Baltimore have agreed to let a religious-cult member charged with starving her baby son to death withdraw her guilty plea if the child is resurrected. Ria Ramkissoon, 22, kept the boy's body packed in mothballs for months because she thought he would come back to life.

FEBRUARY 10

NORTH CAROLINA: HO, HO, HO. Times are tough all over. Nicole Mary Scarpone, 26, was arrested for burglary after forcing herself into an apartment — and asking three men inside to give her $10 in exchange for sex, police said. Police further stated that Scarpone "indicated that she just showed up to make some quick money."

FEBRUARY 11

FLORIDA: It has been reported that police in Orlando thought they could be "flushing" out a group of terrorists. Why? Well, they spotted a trailer marked with anti-government messages and a warning to "Open At Your Risk." They evacuated nearby buildings while a bomb squad officer gingerly went inside where he discovered two toilets and no terrorists.

FEBRUARY 12

CONNECTICUT: Talk about having a bad day! A man who robbed a Darien bank wrecked his getaway car and then took a bus and taxi home, only to find his roommate dead from an apparent suicide, said police. David Maksimik, 59, was arrested after he called 911 to get help for his friend. Unfortunately, responding police found the money from the bank robbery.

FEBRUARY 13

NEW YORK: He sounds perverted. An accomplished Long Island magician and photographer was recently charged with using hidden cameras to record women and girls as they changed costumes during photo shoots at his home. Robert Infantino, 50, who bills himself as Long Island's favorite magician was charged with three counts of unlawful surveillance after police said he taped a mother and her two daughters, ages 10 and 14 at his home in July, 2008.

FEBRUARY 14

TEXAS: Drunk? Guess this fellow needed an energy boost for the night he had planned. A wheelchair bound robber ignored a cash register at a Dallas 7-Eleven, snatching 10 packets of condoms and an energy drink. Cops said the suspect was probably drunk.

FEBRUARY 15

TENNESSEE: A Tennessee man who had a stroke thought that he was minutes from dying. So, he confessed to a 1977 murder. However, James Brewer didn't die and now faces a murder charge! There's no statute of limitations on murder.

FEBRUARY 16

CALIFORNIA: Dangerous duo. Two elderly Los Angeles women were sentenced to life in prison without the possibility of parole for murdering two indigent men and then collecting on their insurance policies that the women had taken out on their lives. The evidence at trial revealed that the women, Helen Golay, age 77, and Olga Rufterschmidt, 75, a native of Hungary, befriended the two men, took out life insurance policies on them and then staged their deaths to look like hit and run auto accidents. Prosecutors alleged that the women collected $2.8 million from the scheme. Wow! Lonely old men can be easy dupes.

FEBRUARY 17

FLORIDA: Dope! We learn that Michael Scott, 19, was recently arrested in a Pensacola Home Depot store while trying to purchase a bolt cutter. Why? Michael had just escaped police custody moments earlier and he was still wearing handcuffs according to a police report. Suspicious employees called the police.

FEBRUARY 18

LOUISIANA: No love in this one. A Louisiana man who offered to help his girlfriend renovate her home landed in trouble with her – and the police too – when he used $10,000 worth of stolen cabinets for the job. He also used carpet that he had ripped up from another burglarized home.

FEBRUARY 19

MICHIGAN: We wonder whether the sex act was missionary or doggie style! Jason Savage, 29, was sentenced to 90 days in jail for performing a sex act with a vacuum at a Saginaw car wash. Appalled witnesses immediately called police. Savage pleaded no contest to indecent exposure. He has been ordered to submit to drug testing.

FEBRUARY 20

FLORIDA; Only in Florida...or maybe Haiti! In Deltona, Florida a voodoo doll with a picture of a Deltona City Commissioner's face on it was found in a woman's yard. The 5 inch doll found in Zenaida Denizac's yard had several pins stuck in it. Denizac's husband found the doll on their front lawn near the mailbox. He at first thought it was trash but realizing it was a voodoo doll he called police.

Police say it is too early in their investigation to determine whether this was a hate crime.

FEBRUARY 21

MISSOURI: She was stupid. She should have planned her escape route before committing the theft. St. Louis police were able to stop the woman, who allegedly tried to shoplift $1,200 worth of goods from a store, when she became confused and kept trying to go out the automatic "in" door. She then became agitated which drew authorities' attention.

FEBRUARY 22

FLORIDA: Potato salad? A Tampa woman grabbed a knife and threatened her 80 year old father when he refused to share his potato salad at dinner. His meal was interrupted when Karen Henry waved a blade in his face. Her dad grabbed a chair to defend himself. 911 was called. Karen was arrested.

FEBRUARY 23

FLORIDA: A Miami Gardens woman was issued a red light camera ticket three months after she died. Her sister Irene Lieberman, a County Commissioner, attempted to clear up the matter. Unfortunately, she learned, to her dismay, that death is not on the list of exceptions that allow the ticket to be quashed. But, collecting from the dead is pretty difficult.

FEBRUARY 24

FLORIDA: This officer could not get all his viewing accomplished during his regular eight hour shift. Police Detective

William Burris was recently suspended from the force for 45 days. Why? He was suspended after often filing for overtime after his regular shift. During the overtime he sat around the office viewing pornography on a city owned computer.

FEBRUARY 25

MISSISSIPPI: He should have stuck with the cold cuts. A Mississippi man, Robert Davis, was fatally burned after breaking into a bar. While in the bar he attempted to cook himself some food but set the building on fire. He sustained severe burns in the fire and died two days later.

FEBRUARY 26

FLORIDA: No T.P! A customer at a Florida gas station walked into the bathroom and emerged minutes later shouting, "You don't have any toilet paper!" and began pummeling the station's owner. Police arrived on the scene and arrested the man. Police said, "The PO'd customer hit the owner with fists and whatever else he could grab."

FEBRUARY 27

NEW JERSEY: Idiot. Police in Englewood report that a man called 911 and reported a robbery after a gas station attendant wouldn't give him his money back for an unopened box of condoms. Police charged Kadien Jackson, 21, with making a false report. Officials had responded quickly to the call on a

Sunday night and found the gas station employee who fit the description of the robber given by the caller.

FEBRUARY 28

TEXAS: Too young to be a designated driver? In mid-August, 2008, a 35-year-old Texas woman was arrested after she made her 12 year old daughter drive her to a bar outside Houston. Police spotted the obviously unlicensed girl driving erratically. She told police she had dropped off her mom who was afraid to drive drunk.

Stories for March

MARCH 1

NEW ZEALAND: The worm turns. A New Zealander who raped a woman in his car was arrested after he fell asleep and she drove him to a police station. Vipul Sharma, 22, was convicted in November, 2008, of abduction and rape for the attack which occurred in 2006 in an Auckland park. After the assault he fell asleep – and woke up only after the victim had driven to the city's central police station. Police Detective Simon Welsh said, "She showed a lot of bravery and common sense. I have nothing but respect for what she has endured."

MARCH 2

WASHINGTON: What a numbskull! A man in Washington State thought it would be funny to stroll into a bank on Halloween of 2008, dressed as a terror bomber complete with fake explosives wrapped around his body. The police disagreed. The 39 year old man donned a white robe, turban and a very realistic-looking fake bomb when he walked into the U.S. Bank branch in Kennewick, only to be stopped by police on his way out and ordered to lie on the ground. Police said the man, who may face charges, thought it would be a funny gag. Not funny, already!

MARCH 3

OHIO: …It took her long enough. An Ohio woman who was cleaning out her home found a book that she had checked out of a Tulsa, Oklahoma, high school library 61 years ago – and mailed it back, with a $250 check to cover late fees. "I sent it back just because I value the education I got at that school," said Martha Jarrett.

MARCH 4

FLORIDA: Oh Poot…An eighth grader in Polk County was suspended from riding his school bus for three days — for passing gas. "It wasn't even me. It was the kid who sits next to me," said purported gas-passer, Jonathan Locke Jr. 15. Polk County school official, Jerome Corbert, said that although there is no specific rule banning flatulence, "There's a rule against disturbing the bus."

MARCH 5

 MINNESOTA: Here's one about an easy arrest. Police did not have much trouble arresting a drunken man after he drove his car up to the gasoline pump at police headquarters and tried filling his tank. One officer said, "It's humorous that someone would be arrested for DWI at police headquarters."

MARCH 6

TENNESSEE: A man on trial for a robbery used his trial lunch break to commit another robbery. We learn that Mark Burgin allegedly robbed a jewelry store of $45,000 in goods while he was on trial for robbing a truck driver at knife point. We learn further that second arrest did not affect his trial because the judge kept the jurors from hearing about it...at least, until after they found him guilty.

MARCH 7

MISSOURI: Sizzle, Sizzle. Police in this St. Louis suburb arrested Damon Perry after a homeowner returned to his house to find the 36 year old burglar frying bacon on the stove. Perry is a suspect in a string of other burglaries in the neighborhood.

MARCH 8

MINNESOTA: A cool arrest? A man was arrested for allegedly stealing Freon from a neighbor's air conditioner and inhaling the refrigerant. Brentyn Krueger, 36, was found slumped over his neighbor's outdoor air conditioner unit, according to the police report.

MARCH 9

CALIFORNIA: Geronimo! A California porn star who is also a skydiving instructor may be in for trouble. The porno skydiver was recently seen in a YouTube video posted online showing him jumping out of an airplane and having sex with a lady skydiver in midair. Police are still trying to discover whether Alex Torres' sex dive broke any law.

MARCH 10

PENNSYLVANIA: Drunk and dumb too. A man allegedly assaulted a police officer who made traffic stop of him for DUI on a lawn tractor. Mark Grove, 44, had a coffee mug full of beer sitting on his tractor. He allegedly told the officer "I'm drunk. Just take me home." He then kicked the officer and, once in the police cruiser, head butted the protective partition between the front and back seat of the vehicle.

MARCH 11

FLORIDA: This story must have a hole in it. A Dunkin' Donuts worker in New Port Richey who took home end of the day unsold pastries has been arrested for grand theft. A manager at the Newport Richey store pressed criminal charges after the employee defied a standing order to throw out the leftovers.

MARCH 12

FLORIDA: Sheriff's deputies are looking for a thief who dressed like SpongeBob SquarePants as he robbed a 7-Eleven in the Orlando area. The police report advises that the suspect did not completely buy into the role because he only wore the

SpongeBob mask. We learn there were no SquarePants worn. Look for the suspect under the sea.

MARCH 13

FLORIDA: A repentant would-be robber who left a MetroPCS cell phone store near Miami empty handed after his intended victim, Nayara Goncalves, 20, calmly told him about her love of Jesus. Israel Camacho, 37, of Coral Springs left her shop in tears. Unfortunately, several hours later Camacho robbed a shoe store a few miles away.

MARCH 14

FLORIDA: A Lake Worth city manager who was fired for undergoing a sex change operation is in trouble at her new job. Why? It has been alleged that she is a homophobe. After being fired Susan Stanton became a hero to the gay and transgender communities, and found a job in the opened minded town of Lake Worth. However after she criticized a gay bar owner over a noise issue, activists called her anti-gay and demanded she be fired.

MARCH 15

FLORIDA: Heard of man bites dog? Well, in this one, dog Tases policeman. The policeman accidently fired a Taser into his own leg after a suspect's dog jumped him. Officer Curtiss Richard reported that he was answering a domestic disturbance call in Key West when he drew his Taser. The dog bit his right forearm causing the self-inflicted wound. The dog, Buddy, a five year old mixed breed was quarantined for ten days. Bad dog….

MARCH 16

FLORIDA: Temper, temper. This one is about a man facing assault charges in Daytona Beach for assaulting his girlfriend with a grilled cheese sandwich. It appears that the assault occurred when a furious Todd Harvey allegedly mashed the sandwich into Amanda Fulford's face. Hungry for revenge, she tried to bite off his tongue. That had to hurt!

MARCH 17

CALIFORNIA: A California man was arrested on human-trafficking charges after complaining to police that he hadn't been paid by a youth -- to whom he had allegedly sold his 14 year old daughter for $16,000, 100 cases of beer and several cases of meat. Police think that the Greenfield girl willingly went with the 18 year old "buyer," but arrested him too.

MARCH 18

IDAHO: Shameful! These guys are giving lawmen a bad rep. An Idaho sheriff is in hot water for having inmates share disposable razors. Now officials are conducting blood tests to make sure none of the jailbirds have contracted a blood borne disease. And a few weeks ago, an Alabama sheriff was arrested for underfeeding his inmates and pocketing the leftover money.

MARCH 19

NEW YORK: Talk about bait and switch! An Amsterdam, New York man was arrested after eating a lobster he bought, then reassembling the pieces and exchanging it for crab legs after claiming the lobster was spoiled. The clever, if amoral, resident of the town near Schenectady had already begun devouring the crab legs when police caught up with him.

MARCH 20

FLORIDA: He supported her all right. A man loved his incarcerated girlfriend so much he shoplifted two bras for her as a gift, police report. Now Johnnie Brown, 29, is behind bars as his girlfriend prepares to get out of jail in a few days. After Brown was nabbed at Walmart he allegedly told police, "She has done so much for me... I felt I had to support her."

MARCH 21

NEW HAMPSHIRE: UGH! Whatever happened to plain old arsenic, you might ask? A New Hampshire woman has been arrested for allegedly trying to kill her husband by dumping half a bottle of eye drops into his tea. But instead of dying, Tonia Peterson's husband suffered only stomach problems -- albeit for two months.

MARCH 22

TEXAS: He really didn't even have to go to jail. A man who would have been sentenced to six months' probation for a petty crime got those 180 days behind bars instead when he fled custody at a Texas courthouse just before his sentencing. Making matters worse James Carroll Franklin led police on a car chase through three counties.

MARCH 23

FLORIDA: Hocus Pocus? A North Miami Beach police officer and a police department employee got into trouble after they allegedly tried to get rid of the town's new cost cutting city manager by sprinkling bird seed around his office as part of a Santeria rite. The duo hoped that the ritual would make the manager quit before he could institute budget cuts. So stupid.

MARCH 24

FLORIDA: After a 47-year-old man was shot in the chest by an AK-47 at an Orlando motel, doctors patching up his wound found a tumor in his lung and removed it. The man who had been shot during a "24 hour party" with hookers said he wants to use his second chance to turn his life around. Ok! First, no more 24 hour parties with hookers…

MARCH 25

CALIFORNIA: As blind as a bat, maybe? Remember the "Mr. Magoo" cartoons? FBI agents in California are searching for the "The Mr. Magoo Bandit." A bank robber, who is bald with thick glasses, like the famous cartoon character, is wanted for a string of a dozen bank robberies between San Diego and San Francisco.

MARCH 26

TEXAS: Frozen armadillo? You don't hear about this kind of crime often. Police in Dallas are hunting for the man who attacked a woman with a frozen armadillo. The man was about to sell the iced carcass as food to the woman before they got into an argument over price. That's when he used the armadillo as a weapon and threw it at her. The 57 year old woman suffered bruises.

MARCH 27

MINNESOTA: Goat Rustlers? Two young girls wearing their pajamas were seen walking along a street late at night leading a goat. They told a police officer who stopped them that he was their pet, he lived in a closet and they sneaked him out for a nightly walks to keep their parents from knowing they had the pet. An investigation revealed that the girls had attended a birthday party at a local petting zoo earlier in the day and had gone back that night to make the goat their own.

MARCH 28

ARIZONA: They say do not rob a bank when you're hungry. A man walked into a Yuma bank armed with a knife, threatened a teller, and walked out with an undisclosed amount of cash. He then decided to spend some of the money on beer and pizza at a restaurant just down the street from the bank. A suspicious police officer spotted him and made an arrest.

MARCH 29

CALIFORNIA: Two burglars, a 19 year old and a juvenile, broke into a home from which they stole 50 compact discs. They thought the discs were blank. However, when they tried to record music on them they discovered that they were filled with child pornography. The burglars called the police and told them how and where they got the discs. The owner was arrested and the grateful police declined to file burglary charges against the burglars.

MARCH 30

MINNESOTA: Here's one about another easy arrest. Police did not have much trouble arresting a drunken man after he drove his car up to the gasoline pump at police headquarters and tried filling his tank. One officer said, "It's humorous that someone would be arrested for DWI at police headquarters."

MARCH 31

FLORIDA: A New York paper recently reported that Michael Dupree broke into a car three years ago in St. Petersburg and stole a bike. He was chased down by the car's owner and two other men. Dupree who is now serving a 12 year prison sentence for burglary and is suing the three men for $500,000 for "psychological disorders" and disabilities he suffered as a result of his take down and beating.

Stories for April

APRIL 1

FLORIDA: KA-BOOM? A Miami woman was arrested after she drew a picture of a bomb and wrote the word "Boom" on her friend's suitcase as a prank before the friend left for the Miami airport. The friend tried to check the bag with the bomb picture on it. This caused a major airport alert. The friend was not arrested but we are uncertain whether she made her flight.

APRIL 2

FLORIDA: Since they did not have a note two men in Brookville used a hand grenade to rob a local bank. The crooks made off with a small amount of cash. However, we learn police may have some "explosive" evidence in this case. The bank robbers did not wear masks and were seen clearly on security video. Morons!

APRIL 3

FLORIDA: Have you ever hear of "freelance stripping?" It has been reported a woman was arrested after she walked into the Baby Dolls gentlemen's club in Clearwater, took off her clothes, got on stage and started dancing for tips. However, the woman,

Natalie Behnke was not employed by the club. It was the real dancers that called police on her.

APRIL 4

FLORIDA: Criminals can be so stupid. This one did not bring a bag with him to the bank he was robbing. Joseph Price, 61, handed a note to a teller at the PNC bank in Okeechobee which demanded that she fill up a bag with cash for him. However, the quick thinking teller said she did not have a bag. Price became confused and fled the bank on a bicycle empty handed. The police report indicated that Price was arrested seven minutes after fleeing the bank.

APRIL 5

FLORIDA: Also, not very Smart. An Orlando man was arrested for allegedly stealing a swan from a park. A witness saw Geffre Smart, 24, take the swan from Lake Eola Park, police report. The witness called police, who followed a trail of feathers to Smart's home. It was further reported that the swan was not injured and Smart was charged with theft and cruelty to animals.

APRIL 6

FLORIDA: Sheriff's deputies arrested two suspected shoplifters at an Orlando Walmart after one of them used a baby's car seat to take a swing at one of the arresting deputies. Unfortunately, the baby was still strapped in the baby seat. Jodie Willis, 25, and

Megan Kelley, 21, were both arrested and charged with robbery and child neglect. It was Kelley's baby who Willis allegedly used as a weapon.

APRIL 7

FLORIDA: A drunken woman stripped down to her bra and panties and took off into the woods after a motor vehicle crash in Port St. Lucie, police report. Angela Ferranti, 25, allegedly told police she wanted to "conceal her scent" from a police dog. Unfortunately for her, a police dog named Kilo eventually sniffed her out. Ferranti was charged with DUI. DUH!

APRIL 8

FLORIDA: Here is a story from the "They never learn file." A man in Volusia County who failed a drug test was arrested a second time after he tried to bribe workers at the drug testing clinic with drugs. The man's test had showed up positive for cocaine and he wanted the results changed. So he allegedly asked a medical assistant if she smoked dope and flashed a few bags of marijuana at her. He was soon arrested.

APRIL 9

FLORIDA: Sheriff's deputies in Okaloosa County, arrested motorist Mila Birkestrand, 47, who allegedly had crack cocaine on her. She said she was not a drug user, but had received the crack from a man in exchange for giving him a ride. The police report said, "She believed the crack cocaine to be legal payment for providing transportation."

APRIL 10

FLORIDA: A church called Saturday Night Live in Lake County has put up an illuminated sign announcing, "Scumbags Welcome!" along a highway. The church's pastor, Moses Robbins, said it's his mission to minister all of God's children. Amen, Scumbags...

APRIL 11

FLORIDA: Hair today, gone tomorrow. Esther Armbrister, 20, allegedly tried to get away with stealing $1,620 from a hotel in Hollywood by hiding it in her wig. Esther glued the hairpiece onto her head with 15 $100 bills and 6 $20 bills stuck under it before police arrested her.

APRIL 12

FLORIDA: Police grilled an East Lee County High School student over his T-shirt, which read, "A friend will help you move, but a real friend will help you move a body." The boy said he had no plans to harm anyone and was allowed to return to class

APRIL 13

FLORIDA: Going Commando? Police in Indiantown arrested a motorist for driving with a blood alcohol level of more than .16 and possessing 20 grams of marijuana. The police report specifically stated that the motorist was not cited for also driving completely naked during her joyride. The suspect had no explanation as to why she was driving without clothes.

APRIL 14

FLORIDA: We learned recently that a Florida lawmaker wants to make it a felony to take photographs of farms in the state without written permission of the owner. The legislation is designed to thwart animal rights activists seeking to document cruel treatment of livestock. The headline read: "Opponents Called it Bull."

APRIL 15

INDIANA: Highway to heaven? Three men and three women at an Indiana prison have been charged with sneaking through a hole in the ceiling to have sex with each other. Having found a security camera blind spot, the inmates would climb into the ceiling, drink homemade whisky, play cards and do the "wild thing."

APRIL 16

CALIFRONIA: Is there no shame left in this world! Looks like the economy is so bad that even thieves are flocking to religion. At least, sort of. Crooks stole a 5-foot bronze statue of the Virgin Mary from a Newport Beach church, apparently to sell it as scrap. The statue was worth an estimated $30,000.

APRIL 17

VIRGINIA: Finger licking guilty! Bernard Wood, 33, was convicted of burglary and grand larceny in Lynchburg after prosecutors linked him to the crime scene by a greasy fingerprint. Wood apparently ate some fried chicken during the break-in and left his prints on a juice bottle.

APRIL 18

KENTUCKY: Life is tough on the outside. A Kentucky inmate who escaped from prison returned later that same day – and pleaded with guards to let him back in. Chad Troy, 21, told police his family urged him to surrender because they feared for his safety. He said he immediately regretted running out the open prison door during a work detail. "I'm sorry about what I did," he said.

APRIL 19

FLORIDA: A Florida woman recently went to her local police station to report that her home stripper pole had been stolen. She contended the 15 foot "expert dancing pole," worth $400, was probably taken by her ex-boyfriend. No suspects have been arrested yet!

APRIL 20

GEORGIA: Murderers should not write songs. Rico Todriquez Wright, a rap artist, was sentenced to 20 years in prison after killing a man and then writing a rap song that detailed how he did it and calling the victim, Chad Blue, by name. "Chad Blue know how I shoot," rapped Wright in the song. And now, so does everyone else.

APRIL 21

INDIANA: Poor parenting and drunkenness are a family affair for this Indiana clan. Police pulled over a mother driving drunk with her 1-year old in the car. When they called the boy's father to pick him up, he showed up drunk. When they moved on to the grandparents, they arrived stinking drunk! Ultimately, the police drove the boy home. That poor kid doesn't have a chance...

APRIL 22

GERMANY: No! It was not armed robbery. A man with no arms managed to steal a TV from a German store. He made off with the 24-inch set using clamps that had been attached to his body by an accomplice. "It's hard to believe that the sight of an armless man walking along with TV clamped to his body did not get anyone's attention," a police officer remarked.

APRIL 23

NEW YORK: This was not holy. A man importing bottles labeled "holy water" from Canada at the Niagara Falls border crossing was arrested when a federal drug-sniffing dog got a whiff of the water. It turned out to be ketamine, an animal tranquilizer sometimes used as an illegal party drug.

APRIL 24

FLORIDA: A Florida fortune teller is being sued for failing to pay back a "spiritual loan" of $13,200. Eumathe Dufrene, 53, said she lent the seer the cash with the promise it would be returned once the evil hanging over her family was lifted. Now it's up to a judge in Naples to determine whether or not the fortune teller, Dorothy Johnson, succeeded.

APRIL 25

FLORIDA: Beep, Beep? A Tampa woman unhappy with her son's grades made him stand at a busy intersection wearing a sign that read, "Honk if I need an education." A goodly number of motorists honked at the 15 year old. We learn, however, that the state child protection agency was not amused at the stunt. They are now investigating the mother.

APRIL 26

FLORIDA: We do not know in what town this occurred, but we learn that a Florida man in the middle of a heated argument with his girlfriend dared her to "go ahead and shoot me." Unfortunately, she did. Robert Lee Gilbert, 57, was shot in the face and died after taunting his girlfriend to pull the trigger on her antique gun as they argued. The girlfriend faces manslaughter charges.

APRIL 27

FLORIDA: Yes. There are fake police out there, believe it or not. Listen to this one. Real Sheriffs' deputies in Orange County, Florida, arrested a pair of imposters, who happened to be brothers, after one of them pulled over a motorist on a highway while driving a real looking police car, complete with lights and sirens. As police deputies were arresting the first phony officer, the second drove up on the scene in his identical fake car to give brother back up. Police report that they were both arrested. FAKERS!

APRIL 28

FLORIDA: Perhaps, it time for him to think about retiring. A Cocoa school teacher who was a finalist for last year's Teacher of the Year Award was suspended for 20 days after he slapped a female student for kissing in a school hallway. The teacher had a clean record and had been on the job since the 1970s.

APRIL 29

FLORIDA: A Tampa police employee was punished after running a personal errand in a department vehicle -- the police helicopter. The helicopter pilot reportedly took the chopper to the St. Petersburg airport to drop off a fishing net to a friend of his.

APRIL 30

FLORIDA: Yikes! A car thief broke into a van in Fort Pierce, apparently not realizing the van belonged to a funeral home. As the thief drove along, he noticed he was sharing his ride with the corpse of a dead 98 year old woman. He became so unnerved at the sight that he ditched the van just two blocks away and ran off. No arrest has been made.

Stories for May

MAY 1

FLORIDA: Old warrants never die. Jessica Pierce, 57, was arrested on a DWI charge in 1977, but did not realize the case was still open until an Orange County sheriff's deputy pulled her over in March of 2011, claiming that there was an outstanding warrant for her arrest. Pierce, who uses a cane and has survived several heart attacks and a stroke, believed that she had cleared up the matter decades ago. It took them 34 years to catch up to her.

MAY 2

MINNESOTA: Trick or treat? A couple in this state was stunned to find a bag of crystal meth and $85 in their 7 year-old son's trick or treat bag. Police say the bag of meth had a street value of $200. Apparently, an older kid had run by the couple's son and his sister and dropped the dope in the boy's bag.

MAY 3

ILLINOIS: Tough Rooster! Police in Benton arrested an aggressive rooster that confronted a woman and a child. Officers detained the cock after what Chief Mike O'Neill described as a brief scuffle. No one was injured, and the rooster was thrown into jail until its owner came to bail it out.

MAY 4

IDAHO: Hungry Howie? An Idaho man was charged with stealing $1,000 worth of cold cuts from a Boise grocery store. Police say the "ham-handed" man went to an Albertson's, loaded up a cart with packaged meats, and wandered out without paying.

MAY 5

FLORIDA: It has been reported that a 48 year old man parked his car in front of the Pascoe County courthouse, pulled down his pants in front of a Pascoe County sheriff's deputy and began to masturbate, according to authorities. Richard Garcia was charged with indecent exposure. Garcia claimed he was just applying hemorrhoid cream. He just wanted to go back to jail. He got his wish.

MAY 6

TEXAS-MEXICO BORDER: Dirty diapers anyone? U.S. Customs inspectors on the border discovered several links of spicy chorizo sausage hidden inside some chunky diapers whose owner, a 21 year old woman, said they were merely soiled. You can't do this! Taking certain agricultural products — including sausages — across the U.S. border is illegal. The woman was fined $300.

MAY 7

WISCONSIN: A bandit floated down a river to keep from being sent up the river. He pepper-sprayed an armored-car driver and then used a very nontraditional getaway vehicle. He ran to a creek that empties into the Skokomish River and floated off to freedom on an inner tube.

MAY 8

IDAHO: Hellcat? Police say a woman battered a security guard, took off her clothes, punched two officers and bit a deputy. Now, Lori Brutsche-Ely, 41, faces several charges. Hailey Police Chief Jeff Gunther stated that the woman was intoxicated Halloween night at the Chester Jakes Restaurant in the Mint Bar when she got out of control. The Idaho Mountain Express newspaper reported that once she got to the jail, Brutsche-Ely bit a deputy and also managed to set off a fire sprinkler, causing her jail cell to flood. She has been charged with four counts of battery, obstructing and resisting arrest and indecent exposure.

MAY 9

NEW HAMPSHIRE: The stupid criminal of the week of mid-November, 2008, was the guy who fled a sobriety checkpoint in this state after handing over his license and registration. Given that they knew the man's name and address, police caught up to him and found marijuana in his car. He was charged with driving under the influence, drug possession and reckless conduct, for almost running over an officer.

MAY 10

FLORIDA: Kurt Fritzel robbed a bank in Charleroi but was quickly apprehended and arrested. Why? A smart bank teller slipped a red dye pack in with the stolen money. The dye pack exploded and left Fritzel incriminating scarlet marks all over him. The explosion also created a red cloud that led police straight to his nearby house before it dissipated.

MAY 11

KENTUCKY: Nine ultra conservative Amish men have been sent to jail after they repeatedly refused to put orange safety reflectors on the back of their horse drawn carriages. The men have reportedly contended that the day glow orange triangles are immodest and they refuse to "pimp their rides," in the name of safety. Amen.

MAY 12

OHIO: Ride by beardings? A mysterious gang of Amish men in Ohio have been riding horse drawn carriages up to the homes of other Amish, breaking into their homes and grabbing men so they can cut off their beards. Officials speculate that it may be part of a feud between sects. Amish gone wild?

MAY 13

MICHIGAN: Chicken as a deadly weapon? Frederick McKaney got into a fight with his mother and stabbed her with a fork. When a neighbor tried to help the mother McKaney hurled 10 pounds of frozen chicken at the neighbor. The poultry left the neighbor woman with a wound that required five surgical staples to close. McKaney pleaded guilty to felonious assault and faces four years in prison. For throwing chicken parts?

MAY 14

OHIO: Inside job, maybe? Thieves broke into a gym in Toledo and stole the entire boxing ring. No one knows how they got the thing out unnoticed, but if it is not recovered, trainers say they will have to cancel upcoming bouts. The ring has been used since the 1970's to train numerous local champs.

MAY 15

FLORIDA: A stereotype of Floridians? We recently learned that customers, who purchase a used vehicle at Nations Trucks in Sanford, receive a $400 voucher good at a local gun store. We learn further that buyers must comply with all local, state and federal laws before receiving their weapons.

MAY 16

OHIO: Hello criminals — you are supposed to dispose of evidence — not create it! Police in Cincinnati were easily able to track down a man who stole a deaf woman's telephone after he snapped pictures of himself with the phone's camera. When the woman got a new phone and downloaded the snapshots from her account there was her thief staring right at her. Why does a deaf woman need a cell phone?

MAY 17

FLORIDA: Seems nothing is sacred anymore. Jonathan Ricci, a Florida man, was arrested one recent Sunday morning after he allegedly tried to steal "a handful of communion wafers" from a priest at a Catholic church in Jensen Beach. During a 9 am mass, Ricci accepted a wafer in the Communion line, but walked away without taking it in his mouth. After a priest's requests for him to accept the wafer, Ricci turned to the priest and grabbed a handful of wafers from the plate and attempted to leave St. Martin de Porres Church. Due to the religious significance of the Holy Communion, a number of parishioners were upset at his callous treatment of their holy ritual and sought to detain him. An enraged Ricci then began to fight with two parishioners aged 82 and 66, respectively. They sustained minor injuries. Ricci was charged with theft, battery, and disrupting a religious assembly. Ricci is a kook.

MAY 18

INDIANA: Richard is one sick puppy! An Indiana man told police he did not know the woman he was having sex with was dead. Richard Elwood Sanden, who had once before been arrested for necrophilia, said he had been seeing her for a few months, and did not realize she was dead until he noticed during sex that she wasn't breathing.

MAY 19

CALIFORNIA: Oooops. A Southern California man could face up to nine years in federal prison after he pleaded guilty to filing false tax returns. The convictions against Albert Bront, 51, will probably also hurt his career and lead to his firing by his current employer. Ironically, Bront is a revenue agent for the IRS.

MAY 20

FLORIDA: Will this marriage last? Gary Newell locked himself in a backyard shed to get away from his pregnant wife. He was then arrested for allegedly threatening to assault her by throwing urine on her after she blew cigarette smoke into the shed to force him out.

MAY 21

NEVADA: Poetic justice? Las Vegas officials hope that their latest tourist attraction will be one of the city's biggest hits. Sin city, next year, will open its new Mob Museum to showcase its colorful past in organized crime. Just to add to the realism, the word "Mob" will be blacked out on the logo — like redacted sentences on court documents. The museum will be housed in a former federal courthouse downtown. Poetic justice?

MAY 22

COLORADO: A man left a "tip" that clearly did not please his waiter. The Lakewood, Colorado resident was surprised to find a topping he had not ordered on his tacos — a small bag of marijuana. The man promptly called police about the waiter and the waiter was quickly arrested. Some tip!

MAY 23

ALASKA: Schultz had too much Schlitz. A motorist in Fairbanks was so drunk that he claimed he had no idea he was driving a stolen car until he was pulled over. Charles Schultz, whose blood alcohol level was more than twice the legal limit, thought he was driving his Chevy Cavalier until a trooper informed him he was actually behind the wheel of a Ford Escort.

MAY 24

OHIO: One desperate woman. We learn that a 37 year old woman charged with having sex with a 13-year-old boy was sent back to jail on a bail violation after she tried to contact the boy by sending him a note wrapped in a burrito. Prosecutors contend that the burrito love note was a violation of the no contact provision of Amy Blose's $20,000 bail.

MAY 25

FLORIDA: Pay back, maybe? A Hillsborough County sheriff's deputy is being investigated regarding photographs of her in a police car smoking what appears to be a marijuana joint and posing with a gun in her mouth. The images of the deputy, Lisa Latimer, were posted on Facebook by her estranged husband, Todd, who says he is only trying to expose the sheriff's department's undisciplined work environment.

MAY 26

KANSAS: YOOUUCHH!! Recently, a Kansas man was stabbed in the scrotum with a hypodermic needle which broke off in the 39-year-old's body. A Wichita police report maintains that the victim told the police the stabbing occurred during an argument with the needle wielder. Investigators further aver that the victim has not been cooperative with officials leading them to believe that the attacker is a girlfriend or former girlfriend of the man with the punctured scrotum. The victim was taken to the hospital for surgery. Police have made no arrests in connection with the assault.

MAY 27

CALIFORNIA: Jiggle Java? Police here have cited three women working in a local coffee house for public nudity for allegedly serving customers while topless at the Quyen Café. There has been an ongoing fight in San Jose between city officials and coffee houses in the Vietnamese neighborhood, where servers many times work in revealing clothes. Here they wore no tops.

MAY 28

OKLAHOMA: Phil Ray Gage, 40, of Oklahoma City, was arrested for mowing his lawn at 4:30 in the morning. Gage was actually mowing the lawn of his next door neighbor who was out of town. He told police he liked to mow in the predawn because he is an early riser. No arrest was made.

MAY 29

MISSOURI: This one is about a carjacking gone terribly wrong. A thief in Kansas City jumped on a woman's car armed with a handgun and demanded that she give him the car. She did not give him the car! Instead, she drove, with the carjacker on the hood, at a high rate of speed to the nearest police station where she crashed into the building. Yes, the "jacker" did receive minor, but not life threatening injuries.

MAY 30

CONNECTICUT: A man was given a two part criminal sentence. The first part of the sentence was three years' probation. The man, Philip Conran, posted a fake ad for a sex party at a neighbor's house on Craigslist. Police became involved, reportedly, after a "parade of perverts" showed up, and one of them groped a girl. The second part of the sentence entails Conran paying for a security system at his neighbor's house. How many "perverts" make up a parade?

MAY 31

FLORIDA: Police in Crestview, Florida recently arrested a homeless man for trespassing. They were able to identify him by his Social Security number. Said number was tattooed on his left leg. Police report that the 45 year old walking Social Security card had been found trying to take shelter at a Crestview housing project.

Stories for June

JUNE 1

MISSISSIPPI: THUD! We learn that a Mississippi woman was shocked when a naked man came through her apartment ceiling and asked her for clothes. Keleigh Townsend denied his request so he grabbed a coat off a nearby hook and ran out. Police say the man was fugitive hiding out in the apartment complex. He had climbed into a crawl space and came crashing through the flimsy drywall was Townsend's ceiling. We learn further that the man was quickly arrested.

JUNE 2

CALIFORNIA: Omar Khan, a California student who has watched the movie "Ferris Bueler's Day Off" 5,405 times has been sentenced for emulating his hero. Khan was charged with breaking into his high school and hacking its computer in order to bolster his grades. He was sentenced to 200 hours of community service and three years' probation.

JUNE 3

NEW JERSEY: Cock-a-doodle-doo. A proposed local law in Hopewell Township would limit mating between roosters and hens in backyard pens to 10 days a year -- and no more than five consecutive nights. "It's a noise issue," said John Hart, a lawmaker who helped draft the ordinance. Great legislative work, John!

JUNE 4

FLORIDA: We learn that a proposed hotel in Sunrise may not get off the drawing board. Why? A ballistics expert made a study and concluded that stray bullets from an existing shooting range a half mile away could hit the planned building and possibly injure those going into or out of the hotel. POW, POW, POW...

JUNE 5

GEORGIA: This one comes from the "How low can you get" file. Police in Warner Robins are searching from a cowardly crook who stole $130 from a 13-year-old girl operating a lemonade stand. Chelsea Edwards was trying to raise money for her 2 year old cousin who needs treatment for a rare intestinal disorder.

JUNE 6

MAINE: The state of Maine has just passed a law that legalizes switchblade knives for amputees who have lost an arm. The policy reason appears to be the fact that since one armed people are not able to use regular folding knives they should be granted a waiver to use the otherwise illegal switchblades. How silly...

JUNE 7

MICHIGAN: Here's a story about trying to save money on gasoline by buying it wholesale and storing it at home. Not a good idea. A man admitted storing gasoline in fuel drums in the basement of his Michigan home in anticipation of higher gas prices. Sadly enough, something sparked a home fire and the fuel drums exploded, as did the man's house. No one was hurt in the explosion and fire.

JUNE 8

FLORIDA: Police arrested a South Plantation High School student after he allegedly brought marijuana laced cookies to campus and shared the chocolate chip delights with two classmates. The suspect's class mates had no idea they were being "treated" to pot. "High School?"

JUNE 9

ILLINOIS: Reckless thieves broke into the Lion House at Chicago's Lincoln Park Zoo and stole $5,000 worth of equipment, including radios and chargers. The thieves were smart enough to not access the areas inhabited by lions, tigers and bears. Oh my!

JUNE 10

PENNSYLVANIA: Oooo la la! It has been reported that a professor at La Salle University in Philly is being investigated after allegations came to light that he hired strippers to take part in a seminar where he and his students partook of lap dances.

JUNE 11

OHIO: Hammered? Christopher Collins of Lorain was allegedly caught on video tape stealing a gavel from the empty courtroom of Judge Chris Cook. "That's a motivated thief to steal from a courtroom," Judge Cook said upon hearing about the crime.

JUNE 12

FLORIDA: A Florida man was arrested for driving under the influence after police asked how much he had to drink. He said two or three -- meaning days. The man's blood alcohol was an astounding .302. The legal limit in Florida is .08. Gosh, how was he still alive?

JUNE 13

CALIFORNIA: The headline read, "She was on a bluff in the buff." The story recounted the fact that police in San Diego had to rescue a naked woman who was stuck on a 450 foot cliff above Black's Beach, a noted spot for nude sunbathing. Police got her down safely, gave her clothes -- and a citation for disrobing in public. Nevertheless, she looks fabulous!

JUNE 14

PENNSYLVANIA: Let it snow? A man in the Philly suburb of Bensalem pulled a gun on another man who blew some snow on his car with a snow blower. "Somebody better move the snow or somebody is going to get shot," Eddie Simmons allegedly said. We learn that cooler heads prevailed and Simmons did not pull the trigger.

JUNE 15

GEORGIA: An activist group here has gone to court to demand their right to carry their guns to church. The group, GeorgiaCarry.org, is attempting to strengthen the Second Amendment right by saying the right to bear arms in church is protected by the First Amendment. A group spokesperson said, 'Why would you not want to take a gun to church?" The NRA must be behind this.

JUNE 16

FLORIDA: This story reminds us that there is a "black market" for almost everything. Three Tampa area men were arrested recently for allegedly trying to sell stolen disposable diapers at an apartment complex. Police authorities surmise that the trio stole the diapers from a local Babies R US and then went to a nearby apartment complex to sell their swag.

JUNE 17

CALIFORNIA: The headline read: "His false teeth came back to bite him." The police in Sacramento arrested a 53 year old bandit because he left his false teeth in the stolen car he was driving when he fled the scene of an accident he had caused. The airbag deployed after he crashed into two vehicles dislodging his dentures which police found on the floorboards of the car. If the teeth don't fit, you must acquit!

JUNE 18

ILLINOIS: The winter of 2011 brought the country a great deal of snow. Here's a story about snow revenge. A Chicago man had setup a surveillance camera at his home. After one of the winter snowstorms his camera picked up a neighbor stealing his snow shovel. He retaliated by using his snow blower to bury the woman's car. It took her four hours to dig her car out. Perhaps, revenge is best served snowy.

JUNE 19

MISSISSIPPI: A police officer in Kiln recently used a Taser to stop an out of control camel that attacked him. The officer was investigating at the home of Donna Berdine, owner of the camel and a zebra, about complaints the camel had attacked two people in the past month. Who needs both a zebra and a camel at their home?

JUNE 20

ARIZONA: In February 2011, police finally captured the Arizona "techno-pirate" who had allegedly managed to insert a 37 second pornography clip into a cable company's local telecast of the 2009 super Bowl. The so called, "flesh flash," forced Comcast to pay out $10 "we're sorry" refunds to each of its 80,000 Tucson subscribers. Wow!

JUNE 21

FLORIDA: CHOMP! We are not certain of the city where this occurred, but we learn that a 15 year old Florida girl is in trouble with police. It appears that the young lady has a fetish for the "Twilight" vampire movies. She was making out with her 19 year old boyfriend in what police called "fantasy biting behavior." The girl told her mother that she had been attacked and bitten while jogging. Of course, the mother was concerned and called police. The girl was forced to confess to making up the attack. Yes, she was charged with making a false report.

JUNE 22

OHIO: Ohio police are looking for a thief who stole an artificial heart. The stolen heart is worth $20,000 and its additional parts valued at $10,000 were stolen from Perfusion Solution, Inc., in

January. Police and company officials maintain they have no idea who the "heartless" thief could be. Yuk, yuk...

JUNE 23

KANSAS: U.S. District Court Judge Wesley Brown of Wichita is 103 years old and one of four appointees by President John F. Kennedy still on the bench. "As a federal judge, I was appointed for life or good behavior, whichever I lose first," brown said recently. When asked how he planned to leave his job, Judge Brown replied, "Feet first."

JUNE 24

FLORIDA: Sheriff's deputies in Okaloosa County arrested a K-Mart employee on Valentine's Day for allegedly stealing a wedding ring from the store. The 1 karat, half diamond Bowtie Bridal ring was valued at $1,399. And we thought K-Mart was in bankruptcy!

JUNE 25

TEXAS: A Texas man beat his boss into unconsciousness after being denied a paycheck advance. The employee, Richard Richards, also stole the boss' cell phone and $500. We learn that Mr. Richards is currently in jail because he has not been able to raise the $100,000 bail set by the court for the assault.

JUNE 26

VIRGINIA: Officials at Hickory Middle School in Virginia suspended a student after he was caught with a bag of dried oregano in his possession. The school declared it an "imitation controlled substance" because it resembled marijuana. It seems unfair, but it did not help that the student's name was Adam Grass. Ironic...

JUNE 27

TEXAS: A mental midget? Nathan Pugh walked into a Dallas bank and demanded money from a teller, police report. The teller said she could not comply unless he showed her two forms of identification. He complied with the request. He was arrested a short time later.

JUNE 28

KANSAS: Erin Go Brah! A robbery suspect was arrested in Topeka after she decided to attend the city's St. Patrick's Day parade immediately after holding up a local convenience store. The 26 year old woman was spotted by police enjoying the parade after they recognized her from security video. Police indicate it was not hard spot her. She was the only one at the parade who wore no article of green clothing.

JUNE 29

FLORIDA: Bad mommy! A St. Petersburg police officer found it necessary to use his stun gun on a 19-year -old woman who allegedly resisted arrest after leaving her 7 month old daughter in her car while she was sunning herself in a nearby tanning salon.

JUNE 30

WEST VIRGINIA: Angela J. Dehart, 23, had just jumped out of her friend's car after an argument and needed a ride home, police report. So, that is when she came upon a hearse, its door open and a casket inside, parked outside a funeral home. Allegedly she gave herself a lift. Police found the hearse and Ms. Dehart a few hours later. An arrest was made. The deceased missed their own funeral.

Stories for July

JULY 1

NORTH CAROLINA: A North Carolina man called police and asked them to investigate the theft of $325 from his girlfriend's bra, where he had been keeping his cash. The police have not yet made a "bust."

JULY 2

FLORIDA: Hold the MSG! A hungry Orlando woman who wanted Chinese food called 911 to place her take out order: pork fried rice, Crab Rangoon and an egg roll. The dispatcher told the woman three times that she had called the police. Each time, the woman persisted with her questions: "This is the Police Department? Uh, OK. I'll also have an egg roll, too. Do you know how long it will be?"

JULY 3

COLORADO: Police were called when a suspicious "device" was discovered. It was a bomb scare at a local Costco. No bomb was found. The suspicious "device" turned out to be a piñata. It is reported that the "device" was defused by several 8 year olds with baseball bats. Wham bam, thank you ma'am!

JULY 4

MASSACHUSETTS: Flim flam? Johnny Butts, an alleged con man, approached William Pace at a grocery store in Randolph and offered to sell him what turned out to be fake gold jewelry. He wanted $100 for the trinkets. The problem with the con? Mr. Pace is not only the police chief of the town; he also owns a jewelry store.

JULY 5

IDAHO: It may have been a case of "quiet rage." They finally caught her! Who? An elderly woman who had damaged $1,000 worth of books at local libraries. It took authorities two years to catch 75-year-old Joy Cassidy who defaced books by smearing them with ketchup, maple syrup, and mayonnaise. In all of the cases the books had been left in the Ada County night drop box. Cassidy was sentenced to one month in jail and is prohibited from going to Boise area libraries for two years.

JULY 6

MISSISSIPPI: What a nasty pervert! A Mississippi man was arrested after it was discovered on surveillance video that he was having sexual intercourse with four prize winning show hogs. Reports further reveal that the man allegedly infected the hogs with a venereal disease.

JULY 7

FLORIDA: Rev. T.J. McCormick, leader of the Coastal Community Church, lived 50 feet above the ground, atop a mechanical crane, vowing not to come down until 1,000 backpacks with school supplies were donated to the children of Collier City. In three days locals filled the 1,000 backpacks and McCormick came down. We wonder how he went to the bathroom for those three days?

JULY 8

WISCONSIN: *Ay Carumba!* A Green Bay woman who had purchased a refurbished vacuum cleaner became frustrated when the machine continually lost suction. Investigation revealed the vacuum cleaner was clogged with two pounds of crystal meth and a kilo of cocaine. Authorities surmise that the $280,000 of dope was placed there by drug traffickers in Mexico. Mexico is where the machine was assembled.

JULY 9

MISSOURI: Guards in Pineville caught two men trying to break into their jail. Actually, the suspects were inmates who had apparently snuck out to buy drugs and do some partying for a couple of hours. However they eventually wanted back in where a warm jail cot was waiting for them.

JULY 10

NEVADA: Buried in trash? This one is really sad. A Las Vegas woman died in a home so packed with clothes and junk that neither her husband, police nor search dogs could find her body for four months. Authorities contend that the 67 year old compulsive hoarder, Billie Jean James, had gone missing. Bloodhounds were brought in but could not sniff her out. Sadly, her elderly husband who also lived in the messy home finally found her amid the trash. The stink was probably too much for the bloodhounds.

JULY 11

IDAHO: What a boob. How about this one? A woman in Idaho has been arrested for allegedly posing as a plastic surgeon and performing breast exams on other women...in a bar. Kristina Ross went by the name of "Dr. Berlyn Aussieahshowan," and got caught after her patients went to a real doctor, police report.

JULY 12

ILLINOIS: Dildo? A woman in Gurnee was arrested for threatening a police officer with what a police report describes as a "clear, rigid feminine pleasure device." Police approached the 56 year old woman after a restaurant complained that she walked out without paying. The woman said she had the money at home, and since she appeared intoxicated, police escorted her home. She walked into her bedroom and came out brandishing the weapon over her head. A police officer knocked it out of her hand before she could hit him with it.

JULY 13

CALIFORNIA: How large were the trees they uprooted? A frustrated married couple in Murrieta, has been arrested for trashing their foreclosed upon home. The couple allegedly poured dye on the carpets, tore out wiring from the walls and uprooted trees and threw them into the swimming pool. They face charges of vandalism, burglary -- and foreclosure.

JULY 14

FLORIDA: The headline read: "This Florida woman had a beef with Walmart." Arlene Kahn bought ground beef there and was shocked to find two prescription sleeping pills in the meat as she started preparing beef Stroganoff. She called police, who said there was no crime and they could do nothing to help her. However, the WalMart store gave her a $40 gift certificate. What a beef...

JULY 15

MASSACHUSETTS: The winter of 2011 has been unusually snowy. Leo Powers of Massachusetts was probably tired of shoveling snow. How do we know? He was arrested for using homemade explosives to blow up snow banks. Police discovered that Powers, 23, was in possession of military grade ammunition. Yes, an arrest was made.

JULY 16

MICHIGAN: What's worse, child neglect or shoplifting? Police in Holland rushed to a department store after passersby reported seeing a crying, shivering infant who had been left alone in a car on a 20 degree day. The police and the mother showed up at the car at the same time. The police found that the mother was pushing a shopping cart full of stolen goods.

JULY 17

NEW HAMPSHIRE: John Coughlin speeding down a New Hampshire road at 102 mph, was trying to get his pregnant wife to a hospital before she gave birth. When Coughlin realized that a police cruiser was chasing him, he called 911. The police officer shifted gears and began to escort him to the hospital. Once at the hospital the officer issued Coughlin a speeding ticket and told him, "Good news: Congratulations on your new son. Bad news: I'll see you in court!" One tough cop!

JULY 18

LOUISIANA: Why did she have to get naked? A woman got into a taxi in Covington and demanded that the driver take her to Michigan. The driver refused, they began to argue, and then she completely disrobed, slid into the driver's seat and raced off in the taxi. Police caught her after a brief chase.

JULY 19

NEW JERSEY: Two drug taking women were shouting so loudly outside a motel that hunters came out of nearby woods and asked them to quiet down because deer were being scared away. The women did not stop yelling. Police soon arrested them for possession of crack cocaine. Oh Deer...

JULY 20

ARIZONA: There's no such bill. A man who has allegedly robbed four different banks around Arizona ordered one teller to hand over "all your $60 bills." He is now known by the police as the "Sixty Dollar Bill Bandit." He is still on the lam.

JULY 21

FLORIDA: A gas station clerk in Immokalee attacked a man with a wooden stick after the customer tried to pay for a six pack of beer with a $50 bill. Renu Zamann, 22, of Lehigh Acres was arrested by Collier County Sheriff's deputies after being called by the customer. The customer told the deputies when he tried to buy the beer with the large bill, Zamann hollered, "You Mexicans have too much money." He then began beating the customer with the stick he pulled from under the counter. Yes, the encounter was caught on the store's surveillance tape.

JULY 22

WISCONSIN: A pipe wielding 32-year -old Milwaukee man set upon a truck of beer, yelling at the deliverymen for bringing "poison" into his neighborhood. The attacker busted up $2,000 worth of bottled beer, although not everyone agreed with him. As he was arguing with the deliverymen, several passersby helped themselves to free cases of the beer. He was not one of Milwaukee's best....

JULY 23

NEW MEXICO: At least one person did not love her. In Santa Fe, a family's pet goat was killed in a drive by shooting. Police said that the gunmen rolled past the family's home in the center of the city and opened fire, hitting Maria, a Nigerian dwarf goat. The owner had no explanation for the shooting and contended people loved Maria.

JULY 24

COLORADO: Gone in 60 seconds. A Colorado motorist pulled over for drunken driving was saddled with a second DUI after he stole a police car. Adam Segura allegedly slipped his handcuffs and jumped into the driver's seat as police interviewed a witness. Police caught him after a mile long chase.

JULY 25

CALIFORNIA: It must have been one hell of a bad date. A Bakersfield woman died after she tried to slide down the chimney of her date's home. The decomposing body of Dr. Jacquelyn Kotarac was found stuck in the chimney days later. The man had sneaked out of the house to avoid her.

JULY 26

GEORGIA: Talk about a tough neighborhood! Thieves stole a TV set from a family unloading it while moving into an apartment in Atlanta, and, in the process shot the dad in the leg and punched his wife in the face. Then, one of the crooks had a change of heart, returning the TV set a short time later. He even apologized to the family, and gave the wounded man's mother a hug — then ran off when police arrived.

JULY 27

WYOMING: Mighty creepy! Two men driving a friend's car in Wyoming were pulled over by police, who found marijuana, syringes, drug paraphernalia, OxyContin — and a plastic bag containing powder that turned out to be the cremated remains of the car owner's grandmother. The owner told police she always kept granny's remains in the car. The men were charged with drug possession.

JULY 28

IOWA: An Iowa man received a beating from a drug dealer after he bought some dope and then asked for change. The dealer tried to explain to the buyer that this was no Walmart, but the man insisted on change. No word on whether arrests were made. Both of them were dope!

JULY 29

CALIFORNIA: To be or not to be? A vexing 400 year old "cold case" ended in a hung jury in L.A when Supreme Court Justice Anthony Kennedy presided over a mock murder trial for Hamlet, accused of stabbing the kin's advisor, Polonius. Hamlet's lawyers tried an insanity defense, but the jury voted 10 to 2 that the Prince of Denmark knew what he was doing, that is, he knew right from wrong.

JULY 30

NORTH CAROLINA: A North Carolina man was arrested after he called 911 to help him find a prostitute. He dressed it up by telling Lexington police that he was seeking "a non-emergency domestic escort." What he received was a trip to jail for misusing the 911 system.

JULY 31

FLORIDA: She hit the trifecta of criminal wrongdoing. A Florida panhandle woman flagged down a police officer to ask for directions. Bad move. Maribeth C. Wilson had an open container of alcohol between her legs and a crack pipe in the driver's side door panel. The can of Four Loko, an alcoholic energy drink had a straw in it. A further search of car turned up three rocks of crack cocaine. Wilson also had no driver's license.

Stories for August

AUGUST 1

FLORIDA: A Florida couple was arrested in November for brawling over the woman's missing false teeth, which police later found behind their TV. "You're going to tell me where my teeth are or I'm going to kill you!" said Louise Deeringer, 56, as she gave chase to her boyfriend, Guy Dugas, with a kitchen knife during an argument police said. Shortly beforehand, Dugas had been giving Deeringer what she told police were "flying lessons" – tossing her in the air and onto the kitchen floor.

AUGUST 2

MASSACHUSETTS: A Holyoke man was arrested after police found more than a kilogram of cocaine hidden in a hollowed out hunk of bologna. The local post office had been investigating suspicious shipments and set up a sting to catch the 30 year old suspect. Did his baloney have first name?

AUGUST 3

PENNSYLVANIA: The report says that the groom wore handcuffs and was in a jumpsuit. Judge Leonard Zito did double duty in his Easton courtroom recently. He first held a hearing for drug suspect Franklin Brandt, and then he presided over Brandt's wedding to his fiancé Takesha Piazza. "We're a full service court," explained Judge Zito.

AUGUST 4

FLORIDA: Convenient for filing her claim! A woman accidentally crashed her automobile into the very insurance office that issued her automobile insurance policy. No one in the building was injured, but the woman suffered minor injuries. No word on whether the agency plans to renew her policy.

AUGUST 5

NEW MEXICO: Descendants of legendary old west lawman Pat Garrett have urged New Mexico's governor to reject a plan to posthumously pardon Billy the Kid. The notorious outlaw was killed in 1881 by Garrett, whose relatives contend such a move would tarnish their ancestor's honor. One of them, Pauline Garrett Tillinghast, said, "We have a tendency unfortunately in this country to glorify criminals." True that....

AUGUST 6

NEW MEXICO: This doesn't sound like "Goodwill." Someone left ammunition, a pistol, a grenade and marijuana in the collection box of a Goodwill store in Albuquerque. The bomb squad had to be called. Bang?

AUGUST 7

FLORIDA: Here's a strange story if there ever was one. A mysterious intruder broke into a Fort Myers home when the owners were away. He took nothing, but he did cover a hallway and a bedroom with feathers. Police detectives report that the pillows in the house were not the source of the feathers for they were all made of foam rubber.

AUGUST 8

NEW YORK: Double your pleasure, double your fun. A witness gave police in upstate New York a very good description of a man involved in a fatal shooting. The problem is the description fits twin brothers and the officers have not figured out which one to charge. Ironically, the twins made it even more difficult for authorities when they came to court dressed in identical clothing.

AUGUST 9

MICHIGAN: This should not have been shared. Hadly Jons of Michigan was serving on a jury when she posted a message on Facebook saying it was "gonna be fun to tell the defendant he's guilty." Unfortunately, the trial was not over. Ms. Jons was dismissed from the jury and faces a contempt of court charge.

AUGUST 10

VIRGINIA: King Solomon would approve of the solution. Raymond Reeder, 39, and his girlfriend loaned $2,000 to her childhood friend to purchase a 1998 Saturn station wagon. When the loan was not repaid Reeder and his girlfriend, who held title to the car, hired a repo man to take the car and chop it in half.

AUGUST 11

LOUISIANA: It has been reported that police in Gonzalez have finally arrested the so called "Brownie Bandit," a thief accused of breaking into the same bakery several times, stealing fresh brownies and leaving behind crumbs and broken windows. Jamon Simoneaux, 18, had a bag full of brownies when he was arrested, according to a police report.

AUGUST 12

OREGON: Dimwit! A man in Oregon dialed 911 for room service. Mark Eskelsen telephoned police from his hot tub at his house to tell police he needed a towel, some hot chocolate and a hug. He is now facing a stretch in jail for abuse of the 911 system.

AUGUST 13

PENNSYLVANIA: Here's one with funny but true names. A man named Kermit Butts, 29, was arrested in the shotgun killing of a man named Samuel Boob in Pennsylvania. The victim's wife, Miranda Boob, is also accused of taking part in the Boob-Butts murder by helping Butts and a third suspect who does not have a funny name.

AUGUST 14

FLORIDA: A recent news article reports that police arrested one Benjamin Franklin Davis in the town of Crestview for allegedly passing fake $10 bills at a Walmart store. The story went on to recount that a Benjamin was arrested for using phony Hamilton's.

AUGUST 15

NORTH CAROLINA: A landlord found an interesting way to get back at tenants who owe him at least two months back rent. He painted the words "deadbeat tenant" on the house. The renters called police. The police declined to charge the landlord, stating that spray painting one's own property is no crime.

AUGUST 16

ILLINOIS: A Chicago man allegedly put up a fake Craigslist ad with his sister's phone number and address, saying she wanted to give away all her belongings. Bargain hunters flooded her Joliet, Illinois home. Her brother was charged with disorderly conduct.

AUGUST 17

FLORIDA: A woman who called her husband and asked him to bring her some vodka was arrested after she attacked him when he arrived home without the booze. When she called, the woman said she had drunk all the vodka and needed more. Her husband did not agree. He came home and took away her car keys. She tackled him to try to get the keys back, scratched him and kicked him in the groin. She was charged with domestic battery by Okaloosa County deputies.

AUGUST 18

OHIO: Jizelle Allen was clocked in her car going 78 mph in Cincinnati. Police gave chase with sirens blaring. Upon hearing the sirens Allen slowed down to the 55 mph speed limit and stopped at all red lights until she reached her home. But when Allen stopped, as a result of running over stop sticks that punctured her tires yards from her house, she refused to get out and struggled with police trying to remove her. She finally had to be Tasered. That got her out.

AUGUST 19

TEXAS: Texans and their guns go together. Burglars broke into the home of Bruce Garner in June of 1989 and stole his H&R nine shot revolver. The thief was never caught but Kauffman County Sheriffs deputies recently found the revolver at a pawn shop and traced it to Garner who is now 59-years-old.

AUGUST 20

CALIFORNIA: Grumpy old men? A 70-year-old shopper at a yard sale was arrested and booked for assault with a deadly weapon after allegedly attacking another bargain hunter with a cast iron pan. Jon Joslin was arrested shortly after hitting his rival over the head with the 5 pound pan, according to police. The two men had arrived early at the yard sale and were walking up the driveway when Joslin first attempted to trip Joseph Brown, 64, say police.

AUGUST 21

FLORIDA: We learn that two young vandals thought that they were leaving a cute love message at a Tampa area high school, but ended up causing $30,000 in damage. Two boys, 14 and 15 years old, respectively, poured motor oil on some decorative masonry blocks to spell out a romantic message for a female classmate. The school, however, could not clean up the mess without removing all the blocks. We learn, further, that the girl dumped the boy who left the message. Nitwits!

AUGUST 22

ILLINOIS: A nauseous school bus driver carrying dozens of children opened the door so he could vomit, but ended up falling out of the bus. The bus continued on without him, crashed, and rolled into a ditch. Of course, the Illinois bus company is being sued by parents. A company spokesman says that safety remains "a top priority." Right!

AUGUST 23

FLORIDA: A 23 year old man who was spied lying naked on the beach in Destin told police his name was Brad Pitt before he was arrested and charged with indecent exposure. The Destin newspaper, the Destin Log, reported that the man had gone swimming and took off his shorts when he got out of the water. A woman with two young children said the man was lying with his legs open exposing himself. When county deputies questioned the man he said he did not think he had done anything wrong and gave a false name. A witness who knows the man said he is epileptic and that he had a seizure and passed out. Weird.

AUGUST 24

CALIFORNIA: August 4, 2009. A man has been sentenced to 15 years in federal prison for selling hallucinogenic mushrooms to a teen that was killed when she wandered naked into traffic. Steve Roman, 31, was sentenced after pleading guilty in April to felony drug charges. He sold psilocybin mushrooms to Victoria Nugent, 17, who walked naked onto US 101 and was hit by a car. So sad.

AUGUST 25

MICHIGAN: Did you ever hear the news that Detroit is a tough place. Here's confirmation. Recently, someone stole the tires off the car of one of the vehicles from Mayor Dave Bing's entourage while it was parked at a condominium complex. "It is a microcosm of a larger challenge that we all have the mayor's aide said.

AUGUST 26

THE AMERICAN SOUTH: Superman comes to the rescue! He has rescued a family facing foreclosure. The family was packing to leave their home in the southern part of the country - the exact location of which they do not wish to disclose -- and when they got to the basement, stumbled upon a copy of the very first comic in which Superman appeared. The comic book is expected to sell for at least $250,000 at auction. The man of steel does it again.

AUGUST 27

NORTH CAROLINA: A North Carolina funeral home has been accused of forgetting to bury a body. Oh yeah, they also left the remains in a hearse for nine days. Police found the body of the 37-year-old woman, who had no next of kin, after someone complained of a foul odor. PEE YEEW!

AUGUST 28

PENNSYLVANIA: Two teenagers were arrested at a Subway restaurant for allegedly passing counterfeit $20 bills that they made on their computers. Daniel Buskirk, 19, admitted that he and Adam Wehr, 18, decided in April 2010 to become counterfeiters in order to cover the expense of repairing their cars, police reported. The pair allegedly used an accomplice, who worked at Subway, to exchange their phony money for the real.

AUGUST 29

MAINE: Will the thief sue? A McDonald's has been sued a few times by patrons who accidently scalded themselves with hot coffee, but now an alleged thief has been burned by the coffee. An employee working at a McDonald's in Portland threw hot coffee on a thief who brazenly tried to steal the cash register. Police arrested the scalded thief, who is a suspect in several other robberies.

AUGUST 30

FLORIDA: Bert and Ernie were not there to help... Just a few days after his duet with Katy Perry was scrapped after parents complained that she was showing too much cleavage, Elmo of Sesame Street fame, was attacked at a guitar store in Winter Park. A man dressed as the Sesame Street Muppet was not happy about the attack and fought back – breaking a few of his attacker's fingers. The attacker was arrested and sent for a psychiatric evaluation.

AUGUST 31

ILLINOIS: Zoom, Zoom. Police Sgt. Lee Martin of Naperville pulled over Lucas Wright for allegedly driving 100 mph in a 50 mph zone. The 24-year-old driver told Martin, "he had just gotten his car washed and he was trying to dry it off." Martin admitted no one in the department had ever heard that one before. Wright still received a citation.

Stories for September

SEPTEMBER 1

OHIO: They say working girls need God's love, too. A former director of the Ohio governor's faith based initiatives office was arrested for creating a Website where johns could post reviews of prostitutes. Authorities say Robert Eric McFadden also helped organize $10 raffles that offered an evening with a hooker.

SEPTEMBER 2

FLORIDA: Was it a "club sandwich?" A 19 year old Florida man was charged with battery for hitting his girlfriend in the face with a sandwich while she drove him home. The blow was so hard, it knocked the victim's glasses off and almost caused her to lose control of the car. One helluva sandwich.

SEPTEMBER 3

CALIFORNIA: Out of the frying pan and into the fire? A seriously injured motorist who survived a crash where his car rolled 200 feet down a ravine in California managed to scramble back up to the road looking for help, only to be struck and killed by a passing vehicle. Police responding to the scene were unaware of the original accident until the victim's passenger also climbed up. The hit and run driver has not been found.

SEPTEMBER 4

ALABAMA: Members of an Alabama fire department are trying to figure out why someone broke into their firehouse and stole the "jaws of life." The thief left behind a TV and two air tanks worth $10,000, but made off with the 60 pound $12,000 cutting device used for getting to people trapped in car wrecks.

SEPTEMBER 5

WEST VIRGINIA: Just give her the brewski, already. A woman in this state loves her beer more than her boyfriend. Angela Amodio, 41, allegedly wanted a cold one so badly that she attacked her live-in guy pal when he tried to hide it from her to keep her sober. She punched him in the face and cut him with a screw driver.

SEPTEMBER 6

INDIANA: An Indiana grandmother accused of biting her six month old granddaughter says she couldn't have done it because she doesn't have enough teeth. Penny Hudson has suggested that either the family dog is the culprit or that the girl did it to herself. Police think she granny is lying through her teeth.

SEPTEMBER 7

COLORADO: A pregnant Denver woman allegedly stabbed her boyfriend to death after becoming angry that he had done the laundry with a buddy instead of her, and after he had complained about her cooking. Michelle Martin started "going off" on Michael Thomas' laundry decision, according to a witness. Police said Martin got even madder when Thomas returned home and the couple began arguing "over food that Michelle had cooked earlier in the day." In the midst of the fight their roommate heard a thud and walking into the bathroom, found Thomas on the floor with a knife wound in the stomach. That must have been some very dirty laundry.

SEPTEMBER 8

ARKANSAS: Will he ever find eternal rest? A former employee of a funeral home in Walnut Ridge broke in one night and began setting up a meth lab in the basement in the middle of the night. Unfortunately for him, he forgot the sheriff's office was right across the street. Police noticed something was amiss when they spotted lights on and arrested him.

SEPTEMBER 9

UTAH: Dang it! Police say a Utah man was pulling up his pants after using a toilet at a Carl's Jr. Restaurant when his pistol fell to the floor and fired, blowing up the toilet and wounding him with shards of flying porcelain.

SEPTEMBER 10

FLORIDA: A Tampa man allegedly killed his roommate and then drank his blood so police wouldn't catch him, according to police detectives. Mauricio Mendez Lopez, 42, was caught after a witness saw him holding the glass he used to drink the blood while screaming, "This is my secret!" The witness also told police that in Mexico, killers often drink the blood of their victims thinking that it will keep police from catching them. UGH!

SEPTEMBER 11

PENNSYLVANIA: How dare you have no money for me to steal! A bank robber in this state was so furious when told that the tellers' tills were empty, he threatened to file a complaint with management before fleeing. When the robber walked in, the tellers were on a shift change and waiting for their cash drawers to be filled. The indignant but hapless robber was caught 10 blocks away.

SEPTEMBER 12

CALIFORNIA: If you're going to pretend to be a police you better know the real ones. Antonio Martinez, driving a car outfitted with flashing lights and speakers, tried to pull over a car driven by a person who looked like an easy mark in Oakland, apparently to rob him. However, the driver of that car was an undercover police officer, who promptly arrested him. El stupido!

SEPTEMBER 13

FLORIDA: Here's one about a thief who must think that it costs too much to smoke. When told by a clerk in a St. Petersburg convenience store that the cheapest pack of cigarettes they sold cost $4, he pulled out a knife and demanded the cigs. He then left $2.35 on the counter, shook both the clerk's hands and the hand of the clerk's wife and then fled the store. Police theorize the crook thought $2.35 was a reasonable price for the smokes.

SEPTEMBER 14

FLORIDA: A man was burned in a pre-Halloween undertaking. Ron Nielson, 50, and his wife were setting up a "prank" on their front lawn using gasoline and candles, Palm Bay police said, when he set his clothes on fire. No arrest was made.

Gasoline and candles are never a good combination – especially around Halloween.

SEPTEMBER 15

CALIFORNIA: Would anyone want to buy a black market piranha? A man in LA was arrested for running a ring smuggling the ravenous river fish of Brazil into the U.S. He also allegedly tried to sell illicit freshwater stingrays on the black market.

SEPTEMBER 16

FLORIDA: Are you sure it just slipped off? A Connecticut man arrested for exposing himself to a 14 year old girl at a Walt Disney World Water Park swears it was because his "European-style" bathing suit slipped off. Witnesses told police that Bradford Pellet Biggers, 51, was fondling himself as he lay on a lawn chair about four feet from the girl.

SEPTEMBER 17

PENNSYLVANIA: A woman dressed like a clown in a multicolor wig claimed to have a bomb as she held up a Bethlehem bank. Police nabbed her as she was changing out of her costume in a car. Bozo lives!

SEPTEMBER 18

FLORIDA: An 11-year-old Fort Pierce boy hit his mother in the head with a saw before offering her $5 not to call the police. It wasn't enough, because the woman — who suffered a minor laceration — called police and had the boy arrested for aggravated battery. Tough mom…

SEPTEMBER 19

FLORIDA: How sweet. Man is dog's best friend. David Grounds, 65, lost two fingers while fighting a 7-foot alligator that had clamped its jaws on his wheaten terrier. The West Palm Beach civil engineer said all that mattered was that his pooch, Mandy, got away safely: "I'd do it again," said Grounds.

SEPTEMBER 20

FLORIDA: A man entered a Greenacres Restaurant in Orlando in mid-July, 2009, and asked for change for a $10 bill. When the cashier asked to see the bill, the man reportedly began screaming, "I want change!" Police said the man then grabbed about $40 from a tip box, picked up the cash register and ran out. The officer who arrested him -- still carrying the register while running down the street -- had just come from reviewing surveillance footage at a nearby convenience store, where lottery tickets had been stolen a day earlier. By chance, the officer identified the man as the thief from the footage.

SEPTEMBER 21

FLORIDA: Polk County sheriff's deputies broke up an illegal distillery in Haines City that brewed moonshine in creative flavors, such as peach and apple. I'll bet that hooch was a lot cheaper than orange flavored Ciroc…

SEPTEMBER 22

FLORIDA: He left them flat-footed! A thief managed to escape on foot from pursuing Orange County deputies, even though he had only one leg! The deputies were forced to call in another officer on horseback to try to track down the one-legged man... but he also failed to find the thief.

SEPTEMBER 23

FLORIDA: Doctor Rat fink! A Miami area trauma doctor performing surgery on a shooting victim removed one of the slugs that the police needed for evidence and tried to hide it in his glove to keep as a souvenir. The surgeon initially lied to cops, telling them he wasn't able to remove the bullet, but another doctor snitched on him.

SEPTEMBER 24

FLORIDA: Butterfingers? The family of Charles Gaal Jr., 90, is suing a Winter Park dentist who allegedly dropped tools down Gaal's throat, including an implant screwdriver and a mini- wrench. Unfortunately, Gaal never fully recovered and he died in 2007.

SEPTEMBER 25

PENNSYLVANIA: Career up in smoke! A Pennsylvania teacher mixed her A-B-C's with some P-O-T, say police. Beth Camp, 52, her husband and son were arrested at their home with 72 pounds of marijuana worth about $350,000, police said. Camp is a 25-year veteran of the Williamsport Area School District.

SEPTEMBER 26

KENTUCKY: This fellow was so stupid. The Kentucky "bank" an armed robber tried to rob was actually the offices of the local water district, complete with payment windows. When the man demanded cash, he was told customers had to pay by check only. He fled empty-handed.

SEPTEMBER 27

MASSACHUSETTS: This fellow should eat someplace else. A 26-year-old Massachusetts man has been shot twice within a year at the same pizza parlor. Police say an unknown gunman shot the man three times in the legs and abdomen this week at the Golden Pizza. He is expected to survive. In April, three people shot him multiple times there.

SEPTEMBER 28

SOUTH CAROLINA: Bet that hurt! An employee of a Myrtle Beach Japanese hibachi restaurant used a cleaver to fend off a robber dressed in a gorilla suit, police report. The two struggled, and the employee whacked the monkey-man on the arm with the cleaver. The ape fled with the cleaver lodged in his gorilla suit.

SEPTEMBER 29

IOWA: He should have beat up his father, instead! An Iowa man was recently charged with trying to motivate his son to play football by giving him steroids. Police caught on when the 14-year-old went into a rage and beat up his mother. Investigators found a syringe and 105 pills in the boy's bedroom.

SEPTEMBER 30

FLORIDA: In the end he had no leg to stand on. A paraplegic held up a Florida bank in his motorized wheelchair, and then stuffed the cash into his prosthetic leg. But he had not gotten far when police caught up with him ten minutes later.

Stories for October

OCTOBER 1

RHODE ISLAND: Pope Francis is quaking in his boots over this…. A Narragansett husband said that the 700 gongs he hears each week from the St. Thomas More Catholic Church across the street from his house made him irritable and led to arguments that doomed his marriage. John Devaney, 64, filed a federal lawsuit against Pope Francis and others, and is challenging a town anti-noise ordinance that exempts religious institutions.

OCTOBER 2

FLORIDA: Listen to this one. A judge in Gainesville declined a man's request for restraining orders against President Obama, Heisman Trophy winner Tim Tebow and Jesus Christ. John Gilliand maintained in his court papers that all three of these people were flashing gang signs at him. After the judge denied his request he filed a new request seeking only to restrain President Obama and Tim Tebow.

OCTOBER 3

CHINA: Hey, you two…Get a garage! Traffic mayhem erupted recently in Shanghai, when dozens of drivers starting swerving close to a taxi in which the two passengers were having sex. Several cars clipped each other, but not serious injuries were report.

OCTOBER 4

WASHINGTON: Justin Palmer, 25, of Bellingham, was arrested after he pointed his gun through the window of his pickup truck at a pregnant woman he saw smoking a cigarette. He then threatened to blow her away if she didn't stop smoking. The logic? Palmer takes women's health so seriously he's willing to shoot them to keep them and their unborn safe. Go figure?

OCTOBER 5

NEW JERSEY: She didn't want to ride in a police wagon. A thief with a taste for toys felt so guilty about stealing a young boy's red wagon, she showed up at his house with a new wagon and a stuffed animal. She had been caught on tape, along with a friend, stealing 6-year-old Alex Bean's wagon in the town of Belmar. The video went viral, prompting the woman to make amends. Alex's mother maintains that she has forgiven the thief and will not press charges.

OCTOBER 6

FLORIDA: A Walmart employee in Fort Walton Beach reported seeing a shopper put merchandise down her pants. According to police records she did not take clothes, jewelry, or cosmetics.

Instead, a fishing reel went down the front of her pants, and a flashlight went down the back. The 39-year-old woman was arrested and charged with retail theft. The items were valued at $53.84.

OCTOBER 7

WASHINGTON: A real entrepreneur! A Seattle man made thousands of dollars finding homes for people. The problem, though, was the homes were not his to give. Peter Dance was sentenced to two years in prison for setting up tenants in foreclosed properties that did not belong to him and collecting the rent.

OKLAHOMA: Null sounds a bit dull. An Oklahoma man is in the hospital after chasing down burglars and then being shot by a confused neighbor. The wacky turn of events occurred a few weeks ago when Joshua Snow, of Owasso, saw burglars outside breaking into his car. Snow grabbed his gun and ran outside in his boxer shorts to stop the bandits. However, when he banged on neighbor jimmy Null's door for help, Null blasted him with and a 12-gauge shot gun. No arrests were made.

OCTOBER 8

FLORIDA: She was lucky they didn't "bust" her in the mouth. An Orlando newspaper reports that police are on the lookout for two men who robbed a woman at gunpoint. According to police, a woman sitting in a car was approached by two men with Tshirts covering their faces who demanded money. The woman told them she had no money, so they opened the door and demanded her purse. She advised that she did not have her purse with her. At this point the police report maintains that one of the men then reached in her bra and took $70 and fled.

OCTOBER 9

WASHINGTON: Yo ho, ho, and a bottle of rum…A half-naked man in Seattle went on a boat ramming rampage at a marina. The man allegedly jumped into a 35 foot boat at the Queen City Yacht Club and just started plowing into other boats berthed there. He only stopped after someone fired a broadside at the pirated boat with a shotgun and wounded him.

OCTOBER 10

VERMONT: William Reynolds, 73, was given a $200 ticket by St. Johnsbury police who seized a 2 ½-foot-tall marijuana plant from his apartment. Reynolds maintained he found seeds and grew them without knowing he had planted marijuana. Police acknowledge that Reynolds had no other plants and that there was no evidence he was a marijuana user. Yeah right! You know that once that plant got three feet tall Reynolds was going to become a marijuana user. Old people do this kind of thing regularly.

OCTOBER 11

LOUISIANA: Police report that a drunken man rode his horse into the western-themed Louisiana saloon called "Cowboys" and acted like a movie villain. He actually lassoed a patron and dragged him through the parking lot. The 26-year-old "buckaroo" was soon arrested at his mother's home where he lives with his mom.

Sounds like the mamma's boy needed to let off a little steam…

OCTOBER 12

FLORIDA: Wonder what the bike did to him? A Palm Beach man was jailed after getting into an argument with his bicycle. Richard Bialon, 68, shouted so many obscenities at his bike at a Palm Beach gas station that onlookers called the police. He was arrested and charged with disorderly intoxication.

OCTOBER 13

COLORADO: We've learned that men in Colorado are getting advice concerning drunk driving while they urinate. Bars in the state have installed a device called an "Interactive Urinal Communicator," which plays an anti-DWI public service announcement on a speaker as a patron approaches the urinal. Just the silliest thing I've ever heard of. Wonder if it cuts down on DWI's?

OCTOBER 14

TENNESSEE: A strange-looking man unnerved managers of a small Nashville grocery store, forcing them to accept a mysterious sealed envelope before he left the store. As it turns out, the mystery man was a recovering drug addict who had robbed the InterAsian market and Deli 12 years ago. The envelope contained his written apology for the robbery, along with the $300 he had stolen.

The worm turns…

OCTOBER 15

FLORIDA: KA-CHING! Here's one about dirty money. A DWI and drug suspect in Florida surprised police when $45 fell out of his behind during a strip search. Nicholas Harris, 19, who initially denied he had any cash on him, was described by police as being like a human ATM machine.

OCTOBER 16

RHODE ISLAND: There's gold in them oil drums but you can't steal it! A Cranston truck driver recently pleaded guilty in a conspiracy scheme to steal $430,000 in used cooking oil that he pumped from tanks at hundreds of restaurants in Massachusetts and Rhode Island. Anthony Simone, Sr., 53, was in league with two other men who sold the cooking oil for use in biofuel and animal feed.

OCTOBER 17

FLORIDA: Hiding in plain site? A 21-year-old man with outstanding burglary arrest warrants hanging over his head lied about his age and enrolled in a Tampa middle school and even managed to play for the football team. Julious Threatts played in the season opener after claiming to be 14. He was arrested after another school telephoned and advised he had pulled the same deception there.

OCTOBER 18

CALIFORNIA: A Los Angeles County jail inmate has filed a lawsuit that maintains that he was shot with a "ray gun." Andrew Fuchs contends that deputies blasted him with a military-style heat ray. In his legal papers he claims, "The device fires an invisible electro-magnetic radiation heat beam, causing unbearable pain to inmates." Be aware that Fuchs has been diagnosed with schizophrenia, however, the county had, in fact, announced plans to use such devices in the future. Sounds like Fuchs is already living in the future in his head…

OCTOBER 19

FLORIDA: A Florida man tried to fend off drug charges by advising police that the cocaine they had just found in his butt during a cavity search was not his. Raymond Roberts admitted that the marihuana that was also found in his rump was his, saying: "The white stuff is not mine, but the weed is." Guess he was holding the white stuff for a friend!

OCTOBER 20

NORTH CAROLINA: Cookoo Cookoo, maybe? Ayana Kenyatta Taylor, 21, did not go quietly after she attacked North Carolina police with scissors and had to be Tasered. Taylor, of Union City, New Jersey, managed to get into and drive off in a Fayetteville police cruiser and crashed into several other cars. Police did not reveal a motive for her conduct, but Police Chief Harold Medlock said: "it's not against the law for people to be mentally ill."

OCTOBER 21

FLORIDA: Dummy! A Florida school teacher posted on his Facebook page that he hated his job and students, and dreaded coming to work. It appears he got his wish. He received a five day suspension without pay for his posting. The Manatee County School Board is now drafting rules that will restrict teachers' conduct with respect to online social media.

OCTOBER 22

COLORADO: This is tragic news. Denver authorities have put out a family of its subsidized public housing two days after the main tenant was murdered. Because the victim, Sandra Roskilly, was the only person named on the lease, her mother and her autistic nephew who lived with her had to get out. Authorities at the housing administration said, "We understand the family is under duress, but we will be locking the unit because they have no legal rights." Meanies...

OCTOBER 23

SOUTH CAROLINA: These love birds should have gotten a room, but not one at Home Depot! A couple was arrested for allegedly having sex in a display shed at a North Charleston Home Depot store. Emily Craig, 20, and Shaun Bowden, 31, were both charged with disorderly conduct and Bowden received an added indecent exposure rap when police found him with his pants down.

OCTOBER 24

FLORIDA: A nanny was arrested and charged with child neglect after leaving two children on the side of the road, according to Fort Myers police. It was reported that the nanny, Kristine Bedinotti, 44, was driving the children to the library, but found it closed. She stopped at the bus station to use the restroom. They then went for ice cream. The children said Bedinotti disappeared for 15 minutes, returned and then started acting strangely. She drove erratically, asked a stranger for a cigarette then ran to a house and tried to steal a puppy from the yard. She then drove away without the two children. They walked to a nearby house and called 911.

OCTOBER 25

CALIFORNIA: A San Diego law student who got angry after being forced to retake a class he failed has done what he is training to do – he sued the school. Jackson Millikan has taken the Thomas Jefferson School Law to court after he came back from summer break and was surprised to learn he was re-enrolled in the course he had failed. Millikan, save your money! You are not going to win this silly suit...

OCTOBER 26

OKLAHOMA: When an Oklahoma City mother found a pantsless woman intruder in her kitchen at 6:30 a.m., there was a very good explanation. "My name is Michelle and I'm just having cookies and milk," she said. Police arrested Michelle Stephens, 27, who had allegedly taken off her pants and entered the house through a kitchen window from the patio.

OCTOBER 27

NEW YORK: An upstate man was arrested for DWI, even though he was asleep. Police said they arrested the man when he slipped into a nap while in the drive thru lane at a McDonalds in the town of Newstead. The man never got his opportunity to buy or enjoy a Big Mac or fries. He was instead awaken by the officers and failed a Breathalyzer test. Off you go now lad, off to the drunk tank. No big Mac and fries for you tonight!

OCTOBER 28

FLORIDA: He is too dumb to be a police. Matthew Proudfit, 22, tried to use his law enforcement credentials to prevent Siesta Key police from arresting his friends. But, there was a problem. Proudfit showed police a pocketknife with the words "Law Enforcement" stenciled on it and his application to the

Cape Coral, Florida Police Department. A news outlet reported that he is actually a shelf stocker at a Publix Grocery store. Police report that they confronted three drunken men outside an oyster bar. Proudfit intervened and offered to take the men home. Unfortunately, he was arrested and charged with impersonating a law enforcement officer.

OCTOBER 29

WASHINGTON: Hey, they're here and they are not going back to China. Enough racist rant! A woman was arrested after allegedly entering the Dim Sum King restaurant in Seattle, shouting, "Go back to China," and going on a rampage. She, reportedly, overturned diners' plates, grabbed a soy sauce dispenser and poured it on a man and his baby. She also slapped the police officer as he was putting handcuffs on her.

OCTOBER 30

FLORIDA: How about this one! A Pensacola man browsing for bargains at an estate sale got an unpleasant surprise. While he was looking around, his $450 bicycle was sold for $5. Jim Rodney, 56, explained that he had left his bike — his only means of transportation — near the carport and went inside. When he returned 20 minutes later the bike was gone. The bike was a 21 speed Schwinn Super Sport.

OCTOBER 31

FLORIDA: Why do they all end up in Florida? A man was caught stealing beef jerky and a case of beer from a Walmart at 6 am in Lake City during November, 2010, according to police authorities. Upon his arrest Kevin Robert LeBlanc gave police a false name. After he was fingerprinted at the county jail, authorities learned that he was wanted in New Hampshire for prison breach. Mr. LeBlanc had walked away from a halfway house in December 2009, and never returned. The irony is he would have been eligible for parole in three weeks. The U.S. Marshal's office reports that LeBlanc is a convicted sex offender.

Stories for November

NOVEMBER 1

FLORIDA: Criminal Barbering? Veteran's Day weekend, 2010, the Orange County Sheriff's department became a national laughingstock when it was reported that sheriff deputies and members of the Florida Department of Business and Professional Regulation carried out a series of warrantless raids against local Orlando barbershops that made history for arresting 35 people on misdemeanor charges of "barbering without a license," after having spent several months investigating the matter. A records check revealed that in the last ten years only three people in the entire state of Florida went to jail on such charges. In the instant cases, many of the warrantless sweeps entailed officers swarming the barbershops that had children inside and putting the barbers in handcuffs and "perp walking" them to police vehicles. We learn that one felony arrest was made when one of the raids netted a barber with an unlicensed handgun. We learn further that all the barbershops were in the African American and Hispanic neighborhoods.

NOVEMBER 2

TEXAS: This foolishness even makes Rastafarian beliefs sound rational... A Texas Tech student was allowed to wear a pasta strainer on his head for an official state ID card. Eddie Castillo convinced the Department of Public Safety he should be allowed to wear the strainer based on his religious freedom to worship the "Flying Spaghetti Monster." He stated further, that members of his "Pastafarian" church pray to the Flying Spaghetti Monster to advocate for greater separation between church and state.

NOVEMBER 3

RUSSIA: This one is about an argument that did not end philosophically. A Russian man shot an acquaintance after they got into a very heated debate over the 18th century philosopher Immanuel Kant. Fortunately, the gun used was a small caliber one that did not do much damage to the victim. He will live. It would probably better for these two to never again discuss the great philosophers of bygone days.

NOVEMBER 4

SWEDEN: A driver from Malmo, with $4.5 million dollars in unpaid parking tickets has been crowned the nation's number one scofflaw. Yet, the circumstances appear suspicious. The unidentified man hasn't had a driver's license for three years and he is the registered owner of more than 2,000 cars. Come on! You know this guy must be the owner of a fleet of taxis. Who needs 2,000 cars?

NOVEMBER 5

FLORIDA: Strange things happen in jail. A jail inmate in Hernando County didn't have enough honey buns to pay off a gambling debt and was paid off with a punch in the face. Brandon Markey admitted he lost a football bet with fellow prisoner Ricardo Sellers. Markey said he went to Sellers' cell to give him the bear claws he owed him, but he was short four honey buns. Sellers was not happy about being stiffed on the bet and punched Markey so hard that he had to be hospitalized. Sellers was arrested on a battery charge.

NOVEMBER 6

FLORIDA: Poor Bambi....An Alachua County deputy sheriff found a deer that had been hit by a car and tried to put it out of its misery. However, he wound up prolonging the misery by shooting the deer 17 times. It appears he was told to shoot the deer in the heart, but could not find the right spot and ended up firing numerous shots into the deer's stomach.

NOVEMBER 7

JAPAN: A Japanese man racked up nearly a thousand dollars' worth of damage to a super market when he went on a poking and squeezing rampage, in which he flattened bread, broke boxes and ruined fruit. He told police, as they were arresting him, that the store's staff had been rude to him. A Japanese Knucklehead!

NOVEMBER 8

FLORIDA: Wow! What a sentence. Timothy Raymond Anderson, 51, had been arrested in 2008 on child sex charges by Palm Bay police. In September, 2010, a jury convicted him of the sexual battery charges. Judge Dan Vaughn then sentenced him to 999 years, 99 months, and 98 days in prison. Authorities arrested Anderson after an investigation revealed that he had abused a girl from 1988 to 1991 on a near daily basis, beginning when she was six years old and in his care.

NOVEMBER 9

FLORIDA: The manager of the post office in Cape Coral was so angry about failing a customer satisfaction survey; he had a special cake baked to look like human feces. He served it on what he called "Poopy Day" — to mark his employees' dismal score. Yuck!

NOVEMBER 10

FLORIDA: A Milton woman was arrested for setting fire to her husband's go-cart, boat and Jacuzzi after she caught him watching a Jennifer Lopez movie. Shannon Wriska of Milton is apparently extremely jealous of J. Lo. It is not clear which Lopez film Wriska's husband was watching.

NOVEMBER 11

CANADA: Two "dopes" in Halifax, Nova Scotia were arrested after police stopped their car and found the front and back seats filled with green, growing marijuana buds. A third passenger was found in the trunk, where police said he was riding to make room for more plants. Were they "dopes" or dopers? Pretty much the same thing...

NOVEMBER 12

CANADA: We learn that there is a recent report that medical authorities in Quebec are barring doctors from performing "virginity tests," and any doctor who does could face monetary fines. Researchers uncovered four cases in which doctors were asked to determine whether or not a woman had engaged in intercourse. The College Des Medecins criticized the practice as an intrusion into private lives. No, no to no nookie tests...

NOVEMBER 13

FLORIDA: It was reported that a Jacksonville man recently decided to take a lunchtime bath in the fountain in Jacksonville's Memorial Park. Citizens complained that Wilbert Snead, 61, was also raising a ruckus. A police officer saw Snead shirtless, wet, and covered with soap. His clothes were seen floating in the fountain. A large knife was found in a bag allegedly owned by Snead. When Snead began stomping crayons into the pavement he was arrested with disturbing the peace. What a nut job!

NOVEMBER 14

SCOTLAND: Is his name Dale the whale? A morbidly obese man who used a stolen credit card to purchase $250 worth of pizza failed to appear in court – because he was too obese, his lawyer said. The 21-year-old man, who weighs 550 pounds, pleaded guilty to ordering Domino's four times with the card. Although he pleaded guilty, the judge has put sentencing off to a later date.

NOVEMBER 15

FLORIDA: This guy is no good at his job. A robber in Daytona Beach who accosted a 69-year-old woman driving her car in a Walmart parking lot jumped on the hood and smashed a hole in her windshield. When the robber dropped his gun through the hole the lady picked it up and promptly pointed it at him. The robber, of course, ran for his life. Police were called. No arrest has yet been made.

NOVEMBER 16

CANADA: This story sound flaccid. A 10 foot tall waterfront bush was mysteriously trimmed down into a penis shaped shrub, to the embarrassment of Windsor, Ontario, officials who had not noticed the bush until TV news crews pointed it out.

NOVEMBER 17

FLORIDA: Erick Lee Blanton, 25, asked a man in Fort Pierce to arm wrestle. Blanton lost. The winner then told police that Blanton became upset, got into his pickup truck, drove it across the lawn and ran over a mailbox. Witnesses also told authorities that Blanton pointed a rifle at his opponent. Blanton was arrested and charged with aggravated assault with a deadly weapon and aggravated assault with a motor vehicle.

NOVEMBER 18

NORTH CAROLINA: Checher la femme! We learn that a mortician outdid police and a medical examiner in solving a homicide. Investigators in Spring Lake declared that David Worley, 39, had died in a tragic car accident after his body was found near his crashed vehicle. However, the mortician found stab wounds that the ME had missed. The victim's wife was arrested shortly thereafter.

NOVEMBER 19

FLORIDA: Hey, rent a room! A neighbor called police after seeing a man and woman entering a Key Largo home through a broken window. The couple explained to arresting officers who found them lying on the floor that they were just looking for a spot where they could "make out" in private.

NOVEMBER 20

VIRGINA: It appears that he has issues with women.... Starting in late 2013, Virginia shopping malls are safe from the Virginia "butt slasher." Johnny G. Pimentel of Fairfax was sentenced to seven years in prison for a crime spree wherein he slashed the behinds of women in shopping malls. The attacks began in 2011 when Pimentel cut a 20-year-old woman. He was sentenced in September, 2013.

NOVEMBER 21

FLORIDA: This is one about an 18-year-old who is stingy with his words. An alligator in Naples bit off the hand of Tim Delano. Tim then called his mother and left her this voicemail: "Mom, I have no left hand. Goodbye.'

NOVEMBER 22

LOUISIANA: What blockheads! Some garage sale! Three siblings were arrested after taking water coolers, electronics, music equipment and other large items from a New Orleans area church under renovation and putting them up for sale in their driveway just a block away.

NOVEMBER 23

RHODE ISLAND: BANG, BANG. A 12-year-old boy was suspended from school for three days after he was caught with a gun-shaped key chain. Although the key chain was no larger than a quarter, seventh grader Joseph Lyssikatos was suspended. School officials said they are sticking with their zero tolerance policy against guns and gun related items on campus.

NOVEMBER 24

COLORADO: Shake down or shake up? A man allegedly impersonated an undercover police officer while trying to shake down a drug dealer. However, there was a problem with the shake down. His target was not a drug dealer, but he was a real police detective who arrested the phony cop. The arrestee was 63-year-old Roland Herrera.

NOVEMBER 25

WASHINGTON, D.C.: During the October 2013 government shutdown, a lady was able to lie her way out of a mugging. The lady was approached by a would be mugger near Capitol Hill, and told him she did not have any cash because of the government shutdown. When he demanded her cell phone she told him that she worked of the NSA and that he would quickly be tracked down. That was all the mugger had to hear, and he ran away. The lady actually works for a D.C. nonprofit – and actually did have money on her. Liar, liar, panties on fire....

NOVEMBER 26

TEXAS: Sounds like a case of "selfie" incrimination. Jailers have issued new charges against inmate Paul Reyes, 32, for allegedly possessing a contraband cell phone while locked up in the Bexar County. Sheriff's deputies received a tip that Reyes was taking pictures of himself behind bars and posting them to Facebook. Jailers found the phone in his pants and the charger around his waist.

NOVEMBER 27

TENNNESSEE: Can you hear me now? Danny Smith called Memphis police three times, complaining that he had been overcharged one cent for a can of Heineken beer. Police showed up at his house after the first call and told him that this was civil matter and not a police matter. After his third call police were no longer amused by Smith's persistence and arrested him for abuse of police communications.

NOVEMBER 28

WASHINGTON: Could he have been on drugs or was he just drunk? First he was arrested for trespassing at a Walmart in Sedro-Wooley. A few hours later he stole a car and used it to ram his way into an art museum. The 22-year-old burglar was seen, nude and bleeding, on video cameras rearranging ladders, pieces of an antique stove and other objects in a museum storage area. All of this sounds like nothing more than a call for help-- help for his mental health!

NOVEMBER 29

LOUISIANA: If one wants to steal crawfish tails, they would have to be in better shape than 48-year-old Erich Williams. Police in Thibodaux allege that Williams grabbed a bag of crawfish tails from a grocery store and ran off. However, it is reported that by the time he reached his car, he was so winded he had little strength left to blow into the anti-DWI ignition interlock devise to start his car. Yes, he was soon arrested. My God, Williams is a thief and a drunk, too!

NOVEMBER 30

FLORIDA: In late August, 2010, a man on a motorcycle pulled into a drive through lane at a Bank America branch in midafternoon in Ormond Beach. The motorcyclist sent a small package with a note on it through the teller chute. The note indicated that the package was a bomb and the man wanted money. When the teller backed away from the counter and did not comply with the robbery attempt, the cyclist drove away. The package turned out to be a small tool kit wrapped in brown paper. Police are searching for the motorcyclist.

Stories for December

DECEMBER 1

FLORIDA: How does one handcuff a one armed man? A recent attempted robbery of a Fairwinds Credit Union in Orlando was largely routine. That is, until the suspect's arm popped off. Matthew Meguiar, 26, had entered the credit union moments earlier and handed the teller a note and a bag. The note read: "This is a robbery, bills in bag." The teller filled the bag and tried to pass it through the slot back to Meguiar. The bag was too big and would not fit through the slot. Meguiar turned and walked away without the cash. As he was walking out of the bank he was stopped by an Orange County Sheriff's deputy. There was brief struggle and to the deputy's surprise Meguiar's arm came off. After handcuffing Meguiar as best they could the deputies placed the prosthetic arm on the roof of the patrol car while they questioned witnesses. Meguiar was eventually taken to the Orange County jail.

DECEMBER 2

WASHINGTON STATE: Talk about "out of the frying pan and into the fire!" Earlier this year DNA testing freed a Washington state man, Alan Northrop, after he had served 17 years in prison for a rape he did not commit. That was the good news. The bad news is: as soon as he was released he was served with a $110,000 bill for 17 years of back child support. There is more. It appears unlikely Northrop will be able to win a wrongful imprisonment lawsuit because in Washington State one must prove intentional law enforcement misconduct to prove liability!

DECEMBER 3

TEXAS: Could this have been cruel and unusual punishment? A Texas woman has filed a lawsuit in federal court. She is suing police for making her listen to Rush Limbaugh. Bridgett Nickerson was arrested in Harris County for driving on the shoulder of a highway in October 2010. While the sheriff's deputy drove her to jail, the car radio was broadcasting a Limbaugh show in which Limbaugh allegedly made a "derogatory comments about black people," according to her filed court complaint. Nickerson alleges that she is an African American.

DECEMBER 4

FLORIDA: The headline could have read: "Loko Gone Loco." As many of you know, "Four Loko" is a caffeinated alcoholic drink. Recently, a New Port Richey man drank four bottles and then went on a naked rampage. Police report that Justin Baker, 21, ran barefooted out of the back of his home to a house a few blocks away, smashed a sliding glass door and ransacked the home. He next took off his clothes, defecated on the floor and ripped the oven door off its hinges, according to Pasco County deputies. At another house a woman arrived home to find a naked man smeared with blood, sleeping on her couch. She called 911. According to the *St. Petersburg Times* when deputies arrived, Baker said: "Why am I being arrested? I didn't steal anything." He was charged with two counts of burglary.

DECEMBER 5

GERMANY: Mistaken identity? Female partygoers at a bash in Simmern, Germany erupted in cheers when men dressed as police showed up at their door. Problem was, they were real cops, acting on a neighbor's noise complaint – and not the male strippers thought to be coming to the 30th birthday party. "It was a bit funny for all sides," said a spokesman for the Simmern police.

DECEMBER 6

NEW YORK: Don't shoot your mouth off in jail! Brian Orkiszewski, 49, from Long Island lost his house to his ex-wife in divorce proceedings and was arrested for plotting to kill the judge who gave the house away. Seems Orkiszewski, already in jail for failing to pay more than $30,000 in child support, was arrested after telling fellow inmates he was shopping for a gun for the planned hit. Orkiszewski told inmates he was furious that the house he had shared with his wife and three children had been awarded to his former spouse. Orkiszewski pleaded not guilty to conspiracy and criminal facilitation charges. His defense his attorney said Orkiszewski was, "frustrated, angry, and depressed." The judge in the original divorce proceedings was given court ordered protection.

DECEMBER 7

MINNESOTA: *Cinema Verite?* Spencer Taylor, an overzealous "Joker" fan, who resided in Three Rivers, was arrested after attempting to steal movie posters. Spencer was charged with felony larceny and malicious destruction of property after trying to rip off memorabilia of the Batman movie *The Dark Knight*, at a local theater. Taylor was dressed in a full costume and makeup resembling the "Joker" a character from the film.

DECEMBER 8

NEVADA: Chutzpah! A Nevada Board of Education member was chastised during a public meeting for dangling a piece of jewelry in front of his giggling wife, who was sitting next to him. "I will entertain my wife. I love my wife," said board member Greg Nance. When a deputy attorney general urged Nance to behave properly, Nance replied that there was no law against a wife sitting next to him at meetings. "Therefore, bite me!" Nance told the official.

DECEMBER 9

INDIANA: Police officer gets off one the wrong foot. Tim Pochron had been on the job for only 29 minutes during his first day on the police force when he wrecked his police car. In his defense, the other driver who crashed into him tested positive for drugs was arrested.

DECEMBER 10

NEVADA: Dummy! A man trying to shake down $500 from a Pizza Hut in Nevada outed himself by sending cell phone photos of the restaurant sign he stole that showed his license plate in the background. Of course, using the license number, police were able to track down the 23-year-old man and arrest him.

DECEMBER 11

FLORIDA: This state has more than a number of knuckleheads. Recently, a Florida man was arrested for making false 911 calls when he reported that a slot machine had "stolen" his money. That came two days after a man called 911 five times to ask for help settling an argument with his brother, and just a week after another Florida man called 911 to complain that a Subway sandwich shop had neglected to add condiments to his hero sandwich.

DECEMBER 12

FRANCE: We smell a probable wrongful death lawsuit in this next story. A French prison inmate managed to kill himself despite the fact he was wearing a prison anti-suicide uniform. He somehow fashioned a noose that could support his weight out of the paper jump suit that is issued to suicidal convicts, leaving Paris correction officers wondering how he could have done it.

DECEMBER 13

THE NETHERLANDS: A green-thumbed Dutch man thought his begonias smelled funny. The 73-year-old man was shocked when police told him that his lovingly tended blooms were growing next to a marijuana crop. Police think the illegal plants were placed beside the flowers by local teens. Or, maybe the old Dutchman is in love with Mary Jane.

DECEMBER 14

CALIFORNIA: Here is a guy who watched the movie Heavy Metal too often. A 20-year-old man broke into a small airport near San Jose, and filled his car up with aviation fuel because he thought it would make the vehicle fly and take him to some awesome, rocking worlds. Instead, he just ended up in jail for theft and driving drunk.

DECEMBER 15

ENGLAND: Yuck! A splash and grab robber took off with $10,000 after drenching his victim as she left an English bank. The thief soaked the woman by throwing water over her as she walked out the door, and then helped dry her off before snatching her bag. It is the latest in a string of bizarre thefts that have involved victims being pelleted with paint, peanut butter and dog feces as they leave banks.

DECEMBER 16

WISCONSIN: He really needed to cut his lawn. Keith Walendowski of Milwaukee was so furious when his lawn mower would not start that he took a gun and shot it. Walendowski was charged with felony possession of an unlicensed rifle. In his defense he said, "It's my lawn mower and my yard, so I can shoot it if I want." A witness told police Walendowski was most definitely intoxicated.

DECEMBER 17

WALES: A painter, Gordon Williams is fuming after being fined $60 for smoking in his "workplace" – after he lit up in his van. The Welsh decorator was stopped by police after he lit a cigarette while driving. Williams said, "I was told that, because my van is my place of work, I had broken the smoking laws. It's not my place of work. I decorate houses, not vans."

DECEMBER 18

TENNESSEE: She sounds like a black widow! It appears the original theory about a Tennessee district attorney's mysterious death in a cattle stampede 15-years-ago was just a load of "bull." Officials in Knoxville now believe that Ed Dossett was killed by his wife and then left in a pasture where he was trampled. Raynella Dossett Leath has been indicted for Ed's death. And, oh yes, by the way she has already been charged in the 2003 murder of her second husband.

DECEMBER 19

CALIFORNIA: This one is about a kid with a bright future in law enforcement. A California woman was charged with counterfeiting money and ID cards. Her 10 year old son was the one who turned her in. The child gave police some of the phony cash and told them his mom made fake IDs on her computer.

DECEMBER 20

BOSNIA: Will it turn out to be a "stool pigeon?" Prison officials in Bosnia jailed a pigeon after catching it being used to smuggle drugs to prisoners. "We do not know what to do with the pigeon," said Deputy Warden Josip Pojavnik. "But for the time being it will remain behind bars."

DECEMBER 21

NEW YORK: An accident?? A Long Island woman with a drinking problem killed her husband by running him over with the family SUV as she pulled out of a parking space near their apartment. Maureen Hines, 45, who fled New York after the incident was arrested two days later when police in New Jersey pulled her over for drunk driving. Police say they are investigating whether Hines' conduct was intentional. The facts show that Hines rolled over her husband's chest as she backed out of a space near their apartment. Hmmmmmmm…

DECEMBER 22

CALIFORNIA: This had to have happened in L.A. A man who stole a pickup truck was held up by an armed carjacker at a 7-Eleven. The gunman even forced the first thief to push the truck out of the parking lot when it stalled.

DECEMBER 23

GERMANY: We bet he will save a lot of money when his girlfriend dumps him. A miserly German man let his girlfriend stay in jail for 15 days because he was too cheap to pay her $350 fine. "People are very worried in the current economic climate and they have to make whatever savings they can," said a police spokesman. "He saw not paying the fine as a simple savings."

DECEMBER 24

RHODE ISLAND: Poetic justice, maybe? Pictures from social networking web sites are cropping up in court. Online photos tripped up Joshua Lipton, a 20-year-old college junior, after he was charged in a drunken driving crash that seriously injured a woman. Two weeks after his arrest, he attended a Halloween party dressed as a prisoner. The photos were later posted on Facebook. Prosecutor Jay Sullivan used the photos to paint Lipton as an unrepentant partier living it up while his victim suffered in the hospital. The judge found the photos depraved and sentenced Lipton to two years in prison.

DECEMBER 25

TEXAS: One weird family reunion. Stephanie Ramirez was working in a pizza parlor in Denton, when a robber wearing a wig and sunglasses barged in and demanded cash. As Rameriz took money from the register a coworker tackled the robber knocking off his disguise – and revealing that the robber was Rameriz's father. Police say they do not think that Rameriz herself was in on the robbery.

DECEMBER 26

NEW YORK: Calvin Morett, a 19-year-old high school student in Saratoga Springs was cited for disorderly conduct. His conduct? He showed up at his high school graduation dressed as a 6 foot penis. Officials report that Morett went to court where he stood erect, manned up and pleaded guilty to the charge. For his punishment he was ordered to write a letter of apology to his school. Yes, a stiff sentence!

DECEMBER 27

BOLIVIA: They can do that voodoo that they do so well. Facing a recall vote, Bolivian president Evo Morales got some help from a powerful source: witch doctors! One witch doctor in La Paz, the capital, set fire to a dried llama fetus at the behest of a client, one of several lobbying the spirit of Mother Earth for the president's political survival. It must have worked – Morales overwhelmingly beat back the recall vote.

DECEMBER 28

MAINE: This stolen object was not hard to find. An 8 foot mechanical gorilla that was stolen from in front of a Maine store has turned up hundreds of miles away in a Vermont cornfield. The store's owners were able to track it down when the thief posted a video on the Internet demanding a $1 million ransom.

DECEMBER 29

PENNSYLVANIA: It must have been one heckuva big SUV! Police report that Thomas Jones siphoned off more than $40,000 of gasoline from his ex-boss – by swiping a company gas card and using it to buy 11,000 gallons of gas for himself and others. Jones was arrested in mid-July, 2010, after his former boss at BW Wholesale Florist, Mike Ulrich, caught him in the act. Ulrich stated that after he reported Jones's $43,695.16 in fraudulent fill ups, he spotted Jones gassing up again – and delivered him to the police.

DECEMBER 30

FLORIDA: The headline read: "His sausage was showing." A naked man in the town of Estero was caught on surveillance video stealing $15 worth of sausages, a first aid kit and a package of napkins from the club house of an apartment complex in Estero. The video linking him to the sausage theft showed him sneaking in wearing shorts, which he removed to take a shower before air drying himself.

DECEMBER 31

GERMANY: Buck naked? This German likes his hikes *au naturel*. German janitor Thomas Kranig has been jailed for 10 days for taking strolls without his clothes on. Naked outdoor pursuits have gained a following since the German Society of Nudists joined the German Sports Association.

About the Author

Professor Birdsong received his J.D. from the Harvard Law School and his B.A. from Howard University. He teaches law in Orlando, Florida.

After graduation from law school he worked four years at the law firm of Baker Hostetler. He then entered into a varied and distinguished career in government service. He served as a diplomat with the U.S. State Department with various postings in Nigeria, Germany and the Bahamas.

Professor Birdsong later served as a federal prosecutor. After leaving government service, and before he began teaching, Professor Birdsong was in private law practice in Washington, D.C.

www.BirdsongsLaw.com

lbirdsong@barry.edu

Ordering Information

New books coming soon!

Dear Reader,

If you liked this book, I would greatly appreciate you writing me a review on Amazon or any other book site.

I look forward to sharing more funny stories with you in future books.

Thank you, I really appreciate your help.

Regards,

Professor Birdsong

Winghurst Publications
1969 S. Alafaya Trail / Suite 303
Orlando, FL 32828-8732
www.BirdsongsLaw.com
lbirdsong@barry.edu

Other books by Professor Birdsong:

* Professor Birdsong's 147 Dumbest Criminal Stories: Florida.

* 177 Dumbest Criminal Stories – International.

* Professor Birdsong's 157 Dumbest Criminal Stories.

* Professor Birdsong's Weird Criminal Law Stories.

* Professor Birdsong's "365" Weird Criminal Law Stories for Every Day of the Year.

* Professor Birdsong's Weird Criminal Law Stories, Volume 2: Stories From Around the States and Abroad.

* Professor Birdsong's Weird Criminal Law Stories, Volume 3: Stories from New York City and the East Coast.

* Professor Birdsong's Weird Criminal Law Stories - Volume 4: Stories from the Midwest.

* Professor Birdsong's Weird Criminal Law Stories, Volume 5: Stories from Way Out West.

* Professor Birdsong's Weird Criminal Law Stories - Volume 6: Women in Trouble.

* Professor Birdsong's Weird Criminal Law - Volume 6: Women in Trouble!

* Immigration: Obama must act now!

* Professor Birdsong's 77 Dumbest Criminal Stories.

* Professor Birdsong's Dumbest: Thugs, Thieves, and Rogues.

* Professor Birdsong's LAW SCHOOL GUIDE: Techniques for Choosing, and Applying to Law School